BAFFIN FAIR

Experiences of George Laing,
a Scottish Surgeon, in the
Arctic Whaling Fleet
1830 and 1831

Transcribed, with an historical introduction,
by his great-granddaughter,
June Starke

Edited by Arthur C Credland
Hull Maritime Museum

HUTTON PRESS
2003

Published by

The Hutton Press Ltd.,
130 Canada Drive, Cherry Burton,
Beverley, East Yorkshire
HU17 7SB

Printed and bound by

The Central Print Services,
a Division of the University of Hull

ISBN 1 902709 20 9

CONTENTS

Map of Greenland and Davis Strait showing the places mentioned in Laing's Journal, 1830-1.

PREFACE

Amountain of journals, letters and pictorial records which reflect the lives and experiences of their forebears lie carefully preserved by families the world over as the essence of the influences which have moulded them. They also, of course, form the substance of history. Printed here is a journal which symbolised the Scottish heritage and love of the sea of my father, Thomas Meek Laing, born in New Zealand. The experiences in 1830 and 1831 of his grandfather, George Laing, then young and as yet not formally qualified as a surgeon, have their place in documenting the hard life of the whale hunters who, until the advent of steam, challenged the perils of the Arctic in small full-rigged sailing vessels. The impetus to research and publish his *Remarks* had its beginning in a gathering held in January 1990 at the Wellington Maritime Museum in Wellington, New Zealand addressed by Mr. A.G.E. Jones, Maritime Historian, of Tunbridge Wells in England. The catalyst was a listener's chance comment about the significance of journals of surgeons serving on British whaling vessels.

The tyranny of distance poses difficulties in terms of consultation and research. George Laing grew up in the ancient burgh of Newburgh, Fife in Scotland and although I have had the great good fortune to make fleeting visits to my forebear's roots, my endeavour to place the young surgeon into his environment could not have been completed without the generous help and encouragement of a number of institutions and individuals. Gillian Wilson and Josephine Urquhart of the Laing Museum at Newburgh and Captain John Wilson who is steeped in the history of the ancient town have filled in the background, as has Paula Martin who also uncovered details of the life and career of George Laing; Julie Poole of St. Andrews has unearthed invaluable information towards the identification of his relative Dr. John Laing who in 1816 published his account of his life as surgeon on a whaler under Captain William Scoresby senior, perhaps the most renowned of British whalemen. A most fortunate chance meeting with Mrs. Catherine Lindsay of Tayport gave me the unique experience of visiting with her the haunts of Francis Laing, artist son of George Laing whose watercolours and etchings convey the flavour of that little town as his father knew it. His wife, Elizabeth (Gregory), was Catherine's great aunt and one of his numerous etchings join George Laing's sketches to illustrate this work.

I was soon to learn how very different whalehunting in the Arctic was from sealing and whaling in the Southern Hemisphere of which I have some knowledge. I am conscious that there may be comments in George Laing's text, the significance of which have passed me by, and it is for the experts who have studied Arctic whaling in depth to make any specialised interpretations necessary. In this context my hope is that the journal and Laing's sketches, plus the inclusion of personal experiences of whalemen who endured the great storms in Melville Bay in 1830, and extracted from the *Annual Register* for that year, add something to the documentation of the disaster.

I am deeply grateful to Arthur Credland, Keeper of Maritime History at the Hull Maritime Museum, who has eased my task in many ways. He has been enthusiastic about George Laing's journal and its place in documenting the history of whaling out of Hull, from the day in March 1992 he learnt of its existence. As guide and mentor his encouragement has been invaluable as he has anticipated my needs with regard to research material to a remarkable degree.

To all those mentioned by name and to the librarians, archivists and others whose responses to numerous and wide-ranging enquiries have reached this far away destination with the shortest delay possible, I wish to express my gratitude. The Hull Trinity have granted permission to reproduce Gibson's drawing of Baffin Fair based on Laing's sketches. My thanks too for assistance generously given in New Zealand, go to my niece Heather Goodall for help in transcribing the journal and to my brother Dr. David Laing and other medical men, Drs. Eric Peat, Peter Tuckey and the late John Symondson for their interpretation of the young doctor's treatment of Bourmaster Spence; to my friend Rhys Richards, historian of whaling and sealing in the Southern Hemisphere, and to staff and former colleagues at the Alexander Turnbull Library for their care and continuing interest as I consulted the rich collection which reflects Alexander Turnbull's interest in the sea and exploration. The support and forbearance of my husband as he has smoothed my path is as always much appreciated. My satisfaction lies in the goodwill and encouragement of many people and in the accomplishment of my father's great desire for the publication of the little green volume he cherished.

June Starke,
Lower Hutt, New Zealand.

1a. Portrait of George Laing etched by his artist son Francis (Frank) Laing, A.R.E.

1b. Newburgh on the Tay; a postcard photograph c.1910.

1. SURGEON OF FIFE

A slim notebook carried twice to the Arctic by a young Scottish medical student serving as surgeon on whaling vessels, bears water and smoke stains sustained in earthquake and fire while in the care of descendants half a world away. Its darkened pages encompass observations written in a copperplate hand, as well as the young man's detailed sketches illustrating his experiences of a tempest which destroyed eighteen full-rigged whaleships, and left up to a thousand men stranded on the ice in Melville Bay on the north west coast of Greenland.

Commercial whaling in Arctic waters had begun around the coasts of Spitsbergen in the seventeenth century, and gradually extended north and west to the waters of Greenland and Davis Strait. The surgeon was already an established member of the crew of a whaling ship when, in 1733, the first Act of Parliament regulated the dangerous trade and specified his presence amongst the ship's complement. It was enacted "that every ship of the burthen of two hundred tons have on board forty fishing lines of one hundred and twenty fathoms each, forty harpoon-irons, four boats with seven men at the least (including a harpooner, steersman and a line manager) to each boat, making in the whole twenty eight men, beside the Master and Surgeon, with six months provisions at the least, for such number of men; and every ship of larger burthen, an increase of six men, one boat, ten such harpoon-irons more, for every fifty tons above the said two hundred, together with provisions in proportion" (1).

High standards of seaworthiness were laid down, and before a ship left her home port "proper officers of the Customs" were empowered to make a careful inspection prior to issuing a licence, which incorporated a bounty based on the tonnage of whale oil taken on the coming voyage.

Surgeons were usually employed for single voyages and were often medical students or recently qualified doctors with basic medical knowledge and little practical experience. In the year 1806 a Scotsman, John Laing, responded to an advertisement fixed to the College Gate of the Old University of Edinburgh on the South Bridge. He joined the *Resolution* of Whitby as surgeon on a voyage to the Northern whale fishery serving under Captain William Scoresby, perhaps the most celebrated whaling master of his time. In 1815 John Laing published an account of impressions of "the snow clad coast of Spitzbergen" gained in 1806, and on a second voyage in 1807 when the *Resolution* penetrated further into Arctic waters than any other vessel to date (2).

A generation later, in 1830, another young doctor, George Laing, spurred perhaps by the older man's account of his experiences or even by his personal encouragement, responded to a similar advertisement for a surgeon for the voyage of the ship *Zephyr* of Hull to Arctic waters for the whaling season of 1830. George Laing's journal of his experiences on the *Zephyr* and again on the *Volunteer* in 1831 has been preserved within his family, and was brought to New Zealand in the late 1880s by his youngest child, David Smith Laing, the present writer's grandfather.

The name "Layng" or "Laing" appears in the parish records of the ancient market town of Newburgh near the head of the Firth of Tay in Fife as early as 1663. Descendants of George Laing claim kinship with John Laing who may be identified as the son born about 1773 to Peter Laing, merchant of Newburgh (3). George Laing, the fourth son of Francis Laing (cousin to John and also a merchant) and his wife, Ann Williamson, was born at Newburgh on 26th October 1809.

The end of the eighteenth century and the early years of the new century were relatively prosperous times for Newburgh, an ancient royal burgh which ribbons along the southern shores of the Firth of Tay. John Laing and George in his turn grew up in The Common Way, the long street which bisects the town. Their homes, like every other on both sides of the street, were backed by a long thin strip of "garden ground and orchard" extending to the burgh boundary. From mediaeval times, orchards of apple, pear and plum trees planted here were "a source of considerable profit to their owners"; their cattle and sheep were grazed on common land on the hills above. The town, with a population of close to 2,000, served a rich hinterland producing barley, wheat, oats, beans and potatoes; malting was also carried out (4).

But the trade which occupied the "greatest number of hands" was a thriving hand-loom linen weaving industry. A number of Laing family members were weavers, and the merchants Peter and Francis Laing probably sold the linen webs woven in the town to larger markets in Scotland for purchase by the English market in London and Leeds. However when prices were low, many weavers "accustomed from their early years to handle the oar, as well as the shuttle" fell back on a "seafaring life" (5).

The Firth of Tay was a rich source of salmon returning to spawn in the rivers and streams of their origin. Francis Laing was certainly involved in the salmon fishery as tacksman (i.e. tenant) of two valuable fishing stations immediately west of Newburgh in 1812, and "took other fishings" in partnership with Peter Laing in 1815 (6). These fishing rights would have enabled them to take advantage of the high price which salmon was bringing on the London market. They may also have had a stake in a trade in rock "cut into pavement for the streets of London" from quarries to south of the town "and carried to London by the vessels employed in the salmon trade". (7).

It was at Newburgh that vessels bound for Perth waited for "the flow of the tide" within the Firth of Tay, and cargo was unloaded to allow some ships to proceed further up the river. Newburgh men worked as pilots guiding them up to Perth, and as sailors out of Perth and Dundee; many served in the Navy or as skilled crewmen on whaling vessels of the Arctic fleet, or on long voyages to Pacific waters. There was then, no novelty in men of Newburgh serving as surgeons on these vessels.

Some interesting parallels can be traced in the respective medical careers of John and George Laing and his contemporary and schoolfellow John Lyell, another Newburgh man who served as the surgeon on a whaler operating in North Pacific waters at the same time as George Laing made his two voyages to the Arctic (8). John Laing apparently chose a seafaring life, and shipped out as crewman on a vessel of the East India Company. By 1793 he had obtained sufficient medical training to be examined and passed by The Company of Surgeons, the predecessor of the Royal College of Surgeons of England, to serve as surgeon's mate on an Indiaman. A further examination taken in 1795 qualified him as a surgeon (9). Accumulated earnings from one or more long voyages to the East may have provided the means to extend his medical training, if it can be assumed that he was the student of the same name who matriculated at Edinburgh University for a number of sessions during the 1790s (10). Having married and set up practice in Dumfriesshire, Laing, like other medical men at the time, undertook a further period of study later in his career, when at the age of about thirty five he attended classes at the University in 1806 prior to joining the *Resolution* as surgeon. In February 1807 he was again practising in Dumfriesshire at Isle of Whithorn when he wrote to William Scoresby Jnr. accepting the post for a second season. In the event it was to St. Andrews University that he applied for a Doctorate in Medicine, stating that he had been practising in Dumfriesshire for upward of twenty years: his referees were members of the Edinburgh medical staff (11).

The Faculty of Medicine at the University of Edinburgh was the largest in Great Britain at the time. Clinical experience and courses in medicine and surgery, interspersed with lectures in natural philosophy, mathematics and natural history were offered. The object was to make a medical qualification "a matter of liberal learning and ornamental accomplishment as well as of professional employment ...a particularly effective preparation for a career in the English provinces, the army, the navy or East India Company where the ability to improve was desirable" (12). John Laing's "account of the whale fishery" includes details of life and conditions in the Shetlands and Spitsbergen and "the zoology of the north", and reflects this background.

Indeed a perfect example of the "ability to improvise" and Laing's use of initiative in an emergency is to be found in the measures he took to save a boatsteerer's life after he had been thrown out of a whaleboat "by the stroke of a whale's tail". The sailor was frozen stiff and showed no signs of life by the time he was brought back to the *Resolution*: "His hair was like so many icicles, and the body exhibited every cadaverous appearance. No pulsation was to be found in any part, and I held a mirror before his mouth without producing the least evidence of respiration". Laing tried various means to revive him, and "as the last resource", resorted to mouth to mouth resuscitation and saved his life (13).

The two young men who grew up in Newburgh High Street a generation later undertook their medical training at the Royal College of Surgeons of Edinburgh. In 1829 at the age of twenty two, John Lyell, son of a wood merchant, having just obtained his surgeon's licence from the Royal College, committed himself to four years service as surgeon on the London whaleship *Ranger* hunting sperm whales in North Pacific waters. Within a year George Laing was serving in the same capacity on the *Zephyr*.

Although he was not to receive his surgeon's licence until he had the experience of two whaling voyages behind him, George Laing was soon to test his medical training, though in much less dramatic circumstances than those reported by John Laing. Within a month of embarking on the *Zephyr* the young and inexperienced surgeon was treating the first serious illness for which he was solely responsible in his long career. At the time few details of their medical work were to be found in published accounts of Arctic voyages written by surgeons, but Laing chose to write up this case in his private journal. The details of his treatment of complications arising from injuries sustained by Bourmaster Spence have been found illuminating by present day medics, who have expressed a variety of opinions on the nature of the seaman's illness and the measure of the surgeon's skill.

Surgeons employed on whalers were most likely to treat "colds and coughs ...fractures, dislocations, sprains, bruises, cuts and frost-biting ...", scurvy perhaps or venereal disease "either contracted in England, or the Orkney, or Shetland Isles ..."(14). The surgeon lived in the cabin and messed with the captain and the mate and, with "no routine of duty, no fixed or regular employment to divert his mind" (15) had, on the whole, the easiest and most comfortable time of anyone on board. He was free to take advantage of excursions from the ship when the opportunities presented themselves for exploration, observations on natural phenomena, bird life, hunting polar bear, or perhaps following up chance encounters with Inuit hunters. John Laing with experience of the exotic East, had been "impelled by curiosity, and by a still more powerful motive to visit the snow-clad coast of Spitzbergen" to apply for the post on the *Resolution* (16). Other energetic, sports-loving young doctors (including Sir Arthur Conan Doyle much later in the century) were similarly drawn by the mystery of the Arctic and the adventure the experience offered.

George Laing makes no comment on his motives for joining the *Zephyr*. His journal conveys the impression of a sensible and conscientious young man, but contains no enlightenment as to particular interests. In fact he would have been by no means the only student who sought a berth on a whaling vessel for the eight months from March to October to provide extra funds to help him to complete his medical training, and to gain useful practical experience. The financial reward was not large even with the addition to his remuneration of the very small share allotted to the surgeon of the profit for each barrel of oil landed. Whatever lay behind George Laing's two whaling voyages it was not until 1833 that he acquired the formal medical qualification of Licentiate of the Royal College of Surgeons of Edinburgh (17). Nothing has been uncovered to date as to whether he undertook further whaling voyages: but a hint of more lasting commitment may lie in his journal in the form of a scarcely legible draft of a report on the 1831 season to an unnamed authority – perhaps the owners of the *Volunteer*, Hull merchants T.H. Marshall and Richard Marshall, or Edward Gibson (1787-1859), shipbuilder and promoter of the Arts, of Hull who clearly had access to Laing's sketches to create a watercolour drawing depicting the position of vessels trapped in the ice in Baffin Bay during the great storm of 1830 and was himself a part owner of the *North Briton*, one of the whaleships (see below). He succeeded his father as owner of the Union Dry Dock, was Sheriff of Hull in 1824 and Mayor in 1842.

> *   *   *   *   *   *

Both Francis Laing, George's father, and John Laing died in the 1830s. John, remembered as "a worthy gentleman as well as a skilful physician", is buried in the old parish churchyard of St. Michael's, Dumfries (18). In 1833 John Lyell returned to practice medicine in Newburgh (19). But George Laing and his family disappear from the ancient town, and in 1833 the author of the Arctic journal was living with his mother and brothers at Ferryport-on-Craig, which clings to the headland forming the southern entrance of the Firth of Tay. He was practising as a surgeon there when the General Census was taken in 1841. Separated by two miles of tidal waterway from Dundee, the strategically sited little grey terraced town had been a fortified ferry port and link with the north from earliest times. It was to be renamed Tayport in 1848 by the Edinburgh and Northern Railway Company which rebuilt the harbour to accommodate the first ferries to carry railway vehicles in Europe. From February 1851 paddle steamers carrying passengers, as well as goods and fish wagons, crossed the Firth of Tay from Tayport to Broughty Ferry and completed the most direct rail link between Edinburgh and Dundee (20).

George Laing spent the rest of his life at Tayport which became a thriving little town, home for Dundee industrialists escaping from the smoke and squalor of their mills, as well as the sailors and fishermen who made up most of the townspeople. He remained a bachelor for another ten years and followed John Laing's example by undertaking further medical training in Edinburgh from 1846 – 1848. In 1846 he contributed an article *On the Action of Iodine of Potassium* to the *Medical Times* and was qualified to practice as a "surgeon and general practitioner" from about 1850 (21). In 1850 he married Margaret Butchard Smith, the fifteenth and youngest child of Thomas Smith, a farmer, of Fowlis in Perthshire.

They made their home high above the little harbour enclosed by its seawall, and looked out over the busy seaway where Arctic whalers headed out for the northern fishery, and months later homed into Dundee with their booty to oil the wheels and light the lamps of industry; where East Indiamen came home laden with jute from Calcutta, and sailed out with the produce of the "dark satanic mills" for distribution to widespread markets; the ferries plied to and fro. Here Margaret Laing died of typhoid fever in 1868 leaving four children. The busy doctor took a second wife, Margaret Stewart of Drumsturdie, Monifeith, in 1871. He died on 29th July 1876.

Apart from his journal and a few fragments found in the attic of his Tayport home, basically relating to the Free Church of Scotland, George Laing left no personal records. That his religious beliefs were strong as a young man is revealed in the Arctic journal, as was his teetotalism. Later the courage of his convictions led him to follow the break away Free Church, puritan and evangelical in its teaching, which left the Church of Scotland in 1843. Indeed there are clues that he may have been ordained as pastor to a Free Congregation.

But public records, medical directories and newspapers reveal that the mature George Laing gave faithful service to the small community. At the time of his death, in addition to conducting a thriving private practice, he was serving as parochial medical officer and as Assistant Surgeon to the Fifeshire Artillery Volunteers (22). In a lecture he delivered in 1863 to the young men of Tayport, the majority of whom were sailors, on the subject of "Life Assurance", a "matter to which many had a great aversion", he made reference to 'late shipping disasters', perhaps recalling his experience in the great storm which demolished so many vessels of the Northern Fleet in 1830. The tone of the lecture was "eminently forceful and conclusive" as he stressed that the matter had to be faced in terms of "high Christian principle" as well as of "sound worldly policy" (23).

George Laing's family scattered within a generation of his death, and his descendants are fortunate to have in their possession a tangible link with their forebears in the form of etchings of his parents and of Tayport as they knew it, made by their elder son Francis. Born in 1862 Frank Laing became a colourful figure and respected artist in Dundee at the turn of the century, but was dead by 1907. Generally known as Frank, he was an etcher and painter and exhibited with the society of etchers, elected A.R.E. in 1892, and also showed his work at the Royal Academy, the Royal Scottish Academy and the Royal Scottish Society of Painters in Watercolour (RSW).

Meanwhile in 1889, like so many Scotsmen and women of the time, his brother David, born in 1863, sought a new life and the hope of better health in New Zealand, taking his father's Arctic journal with him. The surgeon and general practitioner who spent most of his life within the bounds of "the silvery Firth of Tay" would surely have been satisfied that his great grandson in New Zealand has followed in his footsteps, and that three of that general practitioner's four children have found their destiny in the practice of medicine.

Summary of the Family Tree: -

1. Peter Laing, merchant of Newburgh.

2. Dr. John Laing, 1773-1832, died at Dumfries. (His cousin, Francis Laing, died c. 1830, merchant of Newburgh.)

3. Dr. George Laing, 1809-1876, died at Tayport.

4. Francis Laing, artist, 1862-1907, died at Tayport. His brother, David Laing, b.1863 at Tayport, died 1916, Wellington, New Zealand.

5. Thomas Meek Laing, 1892-1959, died Napier, New Zealand.

6. June Starke and Dr. David Laing.

14

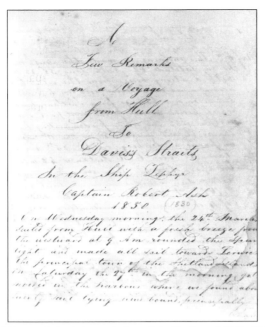

*2a. First page of George Laing's journal abroad the **Zephyr** of Hull, 1830.*

*2b. The author's signature written at the end of the journal 1831-2 along with the name of James Sherwood, harpooner of the ship **Volunteer**.*

15

3. Tayport – looking towards Broughty Ferry; etching by Francis Laing, son of George Laing the author of the journal.

4. Another view across the Firth of Tay to Broughty Ferry; etching by Francis Laing.

5. *View across to Broughty Ferry, the castle prominent; schooner in the foreground .*

*6 View from Tayport with sailing ship and steam trawler **Tayside** of Dundee, built 1899; etching by F. Laing.*

2. WHALING FROM HULL

The British whaling trade opened up and developed midway through the eighteenth century, and for almost half a century after the loss of the American colonies in 1783 the Northern Whale fishery enjoyed a boom period. London had been the centre of the trade until 1750, when enterprising merchants and shipowners in Scotland and the major English northern outports – Liverpool, Newcastle-on-Tyne, Hull and Whitby, began to take advantage of a growing demand for whale oil and whalebone for industrial purposes. Whaling generated trade, and with the support of the government bounty instituted in 1733, made heavy demands on ship repairing, ship chandling, victualling and general port facilities. By 1788 Hull was the leading whaling port in the country.

There were good years and bad years in this highly speculative trade with the ever present threat of total loss, poor catches, or of a clean ship to be weighed against the expense of building, fitting out and crewing of specially built or heavily strengthened existing vessels. The Master was often part owner of his ship, but as a rule the lion's share of the risk was carried by groups of merchants and others who invested in shares sold in units of one sixty-fourth part of the value of the whole vessel. Owners tended to spread their risk by holding shares in more than one ship, and there was often a regrouping of ownership between voyages and even during voyages too, as indicated by records of share transactions in the ships' registry.

A number of factors, political and economic, influenced the growth of the trade. The expanding market for whale oil was reflected in rising prices, while "whalebone", recovered from the great head of the whale, was employed in the manufacture of a growing diversity of goods. This "bone", which had qualities of great strength and lightness, was in fact "baleen", a horny material which forms slender plates covered in hairy fibres suspended from the jaws of Greenland whales (*Balaena mysticetus*) to sift their diet of clione, a shell-less mollusc. A good average sized whale produced about a ton of baleen, recovered from two sets of about 300 plates of up to four metres in length (24).

To some extent the trade in "whalebone" was dependent on the demands of women's fashion; for stay-making, which had become a fine art by the 1770's, for supporting hooped skirts, for frames for ladies' hats and for decorative hair combs. Its flexibility and elasticity made it ideal for the manufacture of umbrellas, twisted handles of various sorts, walking sticks and fishing rods, and among other things for knife handles, framing for portmanteaux, and for carriage backs, sides and springs. The hairy fibres were suitable for upholstery and nets of various sorts. But whalebone had wider and more practical uses. In addition to the items already noted, a hand bill issued early in the nineteenth century by John Bateman and Robert Bowman of the Whalebone Manufactory, South Street, Kingston-upon-Hull, offered:

"Sieves and riddles of every description; nets with meshes of various size, for folding sheep and preventing hares and rabbits from passing through enclosures and pleasure grounds and entering young plantations; slays or reeds for weavers; trellises or guards for shop windows; gratings for granary, barn, warehouse or cellar windows; ornamental blinds of various patterns for house windows; cloth of great durability for the preservation of meat in larders or safes; bed bottoms in place of sacking; …chair and sofa backs and bottoms, in black and white and other colours, after the manner of cane in any pattern; stuffing of hair for chair and sofa bottoms and backs, much preferable to curled hair; brushes of different sorts" (25).

*   *   *   *   *

By the end of the eighteenth century traditional grounds west of Spitsbergen and east of Greenland were being fished out, and whalers were penetrating ever further north and west in search of their catches. Indeed, before John Laing returned to Whitby on the *Resolution* at the end of July 1806, Captain Scoresby had reached the most northerly latitude yet recorded. Leaving the protection of the fleet which customarily sailed loosely in company, he had broken through compacted and seemingly impenetrable ice to reach open sea "almost quite clear of ice" at a latitude of 81^0 30' N. The "situation was singular and solitary indeed. No ship, no human being, it was believed, was within three hundred miles of us. Unquestionably the crew of the ship now occupied the most northern position of any individuals in the world" (26).

But future profits lay in Davis Strait round the southern tip of Greenland, where for a few years more mature and larger whales yielding greater amounts of blubber and whalebone were caught. Early in the season the prevailing north easterly winds generally provided a clear passage to Disco Island on the west coast of Greenland, but only the most intrepid whalers worked along heavier and more persistent ice further than 75 degrees north. However the opening up of new grounds was facilitated by the exploration of Baffin Bay by Captain John Ross, despatched by the Admiralty on a renewed search for a North West Passage. In 1818 the naval vessels under his command, *Isabella* and *Alexander*, led the whaling fleet as they threaded their way close to the shoreline through heavy pack and land ice to the north east. Having named Melville Bay and Cape Melville, Ross left the whalers and headed for the as yet unknown "northern water" before crossing to work down the west land, naming many of the bays and inlets at the top of Baffin Bay, waters soon to become very familiar to whaling fleets. The following year Hull ships reached 77^0 30'N beyond Baffin Bay (27).

In the northern grounds the whales tended to congregate in specific rest or feeding areas, moving slowly northwards as the ice melted. The whalers gathered

20

in Melville Bay, and, as weather conditions permitted, followed them north westward into the "northern water". Here further progress was easier as they followed the coast to Pond Inlet, towards the northern extremity of Baffin Island, and westward again to the more open waters of Lancaster Sound. These were summer feeding grounds and here in 1823 alone no fewer than two thousand whales were secured. But good catches had their price, and crews were returning home three or four months later than formerly after working in an unyielding environment in high latitudes, experiencing conditions which brought them close to the limits of human endurance. A growing number of vessels were wrecked or returned to their home ports clean or damaged. The price of oil was dropping, and as the number of unprofitable voyages grew, so the whaling trade centred on Aberdeen, Dundee and Peterhead, and particularly on Hull as shipowners in other northern ports cut their losses and moved into safer and more profitable ventures.

One hundred and eighty six Hull vessels participated in the Greenland and Davis Strait fisheries from 1754 to 1842, reaching a total of two hundred and nineteen in 1869 when whaling ceased out of Hull. Up to six were captured by the French and sixty six were lost, plus one on the Grimsby register, and two after transfer to Scotland, a total of seventy five well found, full rigged ships. That an experienced master fully familiar with the vessel under his command was the key to most successful whaling voyages, is implicit in the fact that five vessels were lost on their sole excursion into the fishery. Of the fourteen vessels lost from 1843 to 1869 when whaling out of Hull came to an end, seven were lost while under the command of a new master (28).

A fleet of twenty three vessels was whaling out of the port in 1800 and peaked at sixty five in 1819. The tally halved in the next decade, and had reduced to twenty three ships in 1835 after a run of bad seasons and steadily declining prices. The extent of overall decline in the industry can be measured by the fact that Hull was to remain the major English whaling port until just two vessels headed out for the Arctic in 1842. In that season Peterhead, which was moving towards sealing as opposed to whaling, led a total fleet of eighteen with ten ships.

Year by year the fleet had left Hull in an atmosphere of excitement and high hopes for a good season which would have a material effect upon the prosperity of the port. Usually several ships left at the same time. Crowds of people lined the harbour exit to cheer them off, most ships carrying with them garlands of ribbons made by wives and sweethearts to be hoisted on mainmasts far away in Arctic waters in celebration of May Day, and to remain there to become bleached and ragged until the whalers arrived home. But more and more ships were returning "clean" or "dreadfully full" of crewmen rescued from stricken whalers crushed by heavy pack ice. In 1830, the most disastrous in British whaling history, it was estimated that "the capital engaged ...at Hull alone (including wharfs, warehouses, machinery etc. etc.) is probably not less than £400,000; and the individuals it employs are not fewer than 1500". Six Hull whalers were lost, "two more were stove and greatly damaged ...and nearly all the fleet clean"(29). The loss on a clean ship alone was estimated to be about £3000. The harvest totalled only 1,172 tons of oil, the produce of eighty one whales. The industry never recovered (30).

7. The **William Lee** in the Arctic 1831 or 1832: John Ward of Hull, 1798-1849. (Hull Maritime Museum)

8. A unique photograph; the only one known of a British sailing whaler; the **Lord Gambier** seen here in Kirkcaldy harbour in 1860. (Kirkcaldy Museums)

9. Poster advertising the sale of the whaleship **Eagle**, disposed of before the start of the 1835 season. In fact its last whaling voyage was in 1833. After being laid up she was put into general trade. The inventory lists its gear, sails and whaling equipment.

10. A view of Hull from the Humber; the church tower is Holy Trinity, and the building immediately to its left is the pilot office. The south blockhouse at the entrance at the river Hull is on the right. The P.S. **Forfarshire**, of Grace Darling fame, is seen leaving en route to Dundee in 1836 (or 1838); John Ward, 1798-1849. (Ferens Art Gallery, Hull)

12. A whaling surgeon's medicine chest used on board the **Brunswick** of Hull in the 1830s. (Hull Maritime Museum)

*11. Watercolour of the ship **John** of Hull lost at Cape York in the disastrous season of 1821 when nine vessels were wrecked. Thereafter the Hull fleet of sixty or more vessels was reduced to forty and declined steadily with subsequent major losses in 1830, 1835 and 1836. Note the tripods, or "triangles", from which the ice saws were suspended for cutting the ice docks. (Private collection)*

13. Drawing by Edward Gibson, based on the sketches in George Laing's journal, see plates 18-22 and 24.
A representation of the Baffin Bay fair of 1830 with whalers beset, and crews on the ice.
*It is titled 'A sketch of the position of some of the vessels at the late perilous fishery Laying Baffins Bay lat. 72⁰ 14' N. Land 25.0 miles E. DAVIS STRAITS No. 1. **North Briton** of Hull, lost. 2. **Gilder** of Hull, lost. 3. **Alexander**, Aberdeen. 4. **Three Brothers**, Dundee. 5. **William** of Hull, lost. 6. **Traveller** of Peterhead. 7. **Zephyr** of Hull. Signed bottom right E. Gibson 1830.*
(Reproduced by permission of the Warden and Brethren of Hull Trinity House)

26

3. BAFFIN FAIR 1830

One third of the Arctic fleet, thirty three vessels, headed out from Hull in 1830 with the young surgeon George Laing aboard the *Zephyr*, a full-rigged ship of 342 tons burden, laid down at Thorne, Yorkshire in 1796 for whaling out of Hull. Her owners were typical investors, prosperous local people whose occupations indicate interests in industry associated with whaling. Successful whaling masters frequently held a stake in the vessel under their command, and from 1825 ownership of the *Zephyr* was in the hands of her master, from 1815 to 1826, John Unthank, mariner of Sculcoates, Hull, in partnership with Benjamin Stocks, merchant of Cottingham near Hull, and Thomas Shackles, oil merchant of Hull. Until she was sold to London owners in 1845, the *Zephyr* brought them a steady but declining return. Even in 1830, when the average catch for those Hull whalers which had not come home clean yielded forty seven tons of oil, the *Zephyr*'s owners were fortunate. Her hold accommodated seventy six tons, albeit half her harvest of the previous year (31).

The first Hull whaler to head for the north that season had sailed as early as 30th January (32). But it was 24th March before the *Zephyr* slipped out of her home port under the experienced command of Captain Robert Ash, who had shipped out on whalers of the Hull fleet from 1810 before taking over as master from part owner John Unthank in 1827. He made a fast passage to Lerwick to take aboard hardy Shetland Islanders, famed as highly skilled boat-handlers, to crew the whale boats and complete the ship's company of forty one souls, and to rendezvous with the fleet. "Twenty sail were lying windbound" waiting to head north more or less in company.

Laing's Arctic experience began with the observation in his journal that the *Zephyr* had passed an iceberg on 18th April, his first real comment on the voyage. By this time he should have adjusted to life within the narrow, constrained world of the little ship. He had probably found his sealegs like John Laing before him, who confessed that seasickness affected him "so severely as to preclude all possibility of making any remarks previous to our landing in Shetland" (33). Meanwhile the crew would have gone about the preparation of their harpoons, lances, knives and other whaling tools for the fishing, ropes were spliced, lines were coiled and the six-oared whaleboats made ready. The surgeon's task was to issue warm clothing and stores, and pencilled notes in the journal suggest that George was involved in this duty.

But about 20th April he was called upon to care for a sailor, Bourmaster Spence (34), suffering from a shoulder injury sustained after the ship gave a heavy lurch. There is no mention of this accident in George's actual account of the voyage, but his patient's condition was to cause considerable concern for some weeks. His knowledge of medicine and surgery was minimal, and his resources were confined to the medical supplies aboard the *Zephyr*, with perhaps a copy of a text such as *The Edinburgh Pharmacopoeia* to consult (35). Even with the support of Captain Ash with his long experience of the perils of the Arctic, a great sense of isolation and the measure of his responsibility to the ship's company must have weighed heavily upon the inexperienced young doctor. Indeed, more than two months were to pass before he was to have his diagnosis and treatment endorsed by Mr. Aitken, surgeon of the *William* of Hull, a few days before this vessel became a complete wreck on 2nd July.

Cape Farewell, the southernmost tip of Greenland, lay behind the *Zephyr* by 25th April, and she sailed relentlessly north within the perilous waters of the Davis Strait. Five weeks out from the Shetland Islands they were plying the ice edge of the south west fishing grounds. The first whale was secured on 13th May followed by four more during the next two weeks, and a good season seemed to be in store as they made "all possible sail to the North". Disco Island was behind them, and at Black Hook Peninsula conditions were so favourable that "our oldest fishermen never remember of having seen such a body of water at this time of the season".

By 10th June, about a month earlier than usual, some sixty ships were in sight of The Devil's Thumb, an island close into the mainland of Greenland. But a fortnight would pass before the *Zephyr* was abreast of this high pinnacle forming the southern side of Melville Bay, and only then was George able to join his crewmates in observing the whaleman's practice of doffing their hats in salute to the landmark. This custom, and three cheers and a tot of rum for all when a ship was able to quit Melville Bay and enter the "north water" (36), may well have originated with the whalemen who had threaded their way up the coast immediately after Captain Ross's pathfinding voyage in 1818.

Year after year the fleet gathered in Melville Bay as the ships steadily pushed their way along the Greenland land floes to wait for a passage to the "north water" once the middle drift of ice and huge icebergs had moved south in the summer months. There were weeks and sometimes months of backbreaking work edging north and, in an unfavourable season, extreme peril for the ships should they become ice bound. But occasionally there was time for rest and recuperation with excursions on the shores of Greenland, and there were opportunities for the whalemen to visit between the vessels. For example, the observance of two consecutive Sundays is described in a letter written in 1822 to the Secretary of the Port of Hull Society. Thirty ships with crews numbering "1500 men or more" were waiting in ice docks for the north passage to open, when Captain W. Manger of Hull wrote of hoisting a flag at the main royal masthead of the *Cumbrian* of Hull to represent a Bethel (seaman's chapel) flag. Several services, each attended by up to three hundred men, were held on board at which he read a "sermon on keeping the Sabbath Holy, and my father ...and my mate exercised in prayer ...the day was marked with more solemnity than I have often seen in England" (37).

But in 1830 the fleet was never to reach the "north water". By 19th June the leaders had negotiated the narrow channel at the edge of the land floe to reach lat. 76⁰ N where they were waiting to break out of Melville Bay. A long line of ships stretched back to a group of twenty two vessels within lat. 74⁰ N completely beset by the exigencies of the ice. The ships in company with *Zephyr* must have formed the rearguard of a southern fleet, as it was not until the evening of 26th June that Captain Ash made fast to a 'land floe' just to the north of the Devil's Thumb.

Here George Laing became acquainted with the arduous task of "towing" the ship through channels of clear water by boats or "tracking" with men on the ice hauling her along. Each man wore a broad canvas tracking belt called a "row raddie" over his shoulder "like a sword belt" to which they attached the tracking line. If the ice was good they could make about four miles in an hour as they chanted or sang to the accompaniment of "tracking pipes" (38). There is a large body of shanties sung by whalemen to ease such back-breaking tasks. One, the old song "O Logie of Buchan" from the north east coast of Scotland, has a place in George's journal perhaps as his memory of a particular "tracking" routine.

Within a week he was to experience the storm which was to destroy eighteen whalers before blowing itself out. The howling south westerly gale struck the most northern ships on 24th June. The wind, accompanied with drift and hail, was blowing strongly from the south-west by south the previous evening but, as Alexander Kidd, a seaman of the *Achilles* of Dundee reported: "the ice, amongst which she was beset, remained firm: but a sudden and violent irruption took place about one o' clock on the following morning, and the *Achilles*, the *Baffin* and *Rattler* of Leith, and a French ship, the *Ville de Dieppe*, which were in company, were rendered complete wrecks. The *Eliza [Swan]* of Montrose, was severely stove" (39).

The trail of devastation continued as the storm drove south, and its passage is taken up in a letter written by a surgeon serving on an unnamed vessel beset in the ice about thirty miles off Bushman's Island at lat. 75⁰ 30' N:
" ...about 2 p.m. it became suddenly overcast, and blew a strong gale from the S.S.W., accompanied by thick sleet and snow. This awakened our worst apprehensions, and, indeed it was not long before they were realized. At nearly four o'clock, our dock, sawn with extreme labour and upon which all our hopes centred – gave way. This was the general signal for getting our 'traps' on the ice. After each hand got what belonged to himself in safety on the ice, provisions were then hoisted up: for, in the first instance, nothing but self-interest was attended to. The pressure of the ice seemed to be going regularly along; it now passed on to several vessels to the eastward of us; about three hundred yards in that direction lay the *Resolution* of Peterhead, the *Laurel* of Hull and the *Laetitia* of Aberdeen, in one dock; the latter vessel, unable to withstand the tremendous pressure of the ice, was soon upon her beam ends, and in a short time afterwards, her masts went by the board, and she became a total wreck. The *Princess of Wales*, of Aberdeen, was next crushed to pieces, and the ice continuing to press the whole of the night, but in a more gradual manner, many of the vessels were on their beam ends, but again righted: several were crushed many feet above the ice a-stern, and others a-head. We were lying in dock; yet often did we hear our

vessel crack, and, at one time, having heard a crash, though we were ignorant which of the vessels it was, we simultaneously rushed on the ice, a hollow on our starboard bow, produced by the pressure of the two vessels, was the cause of this. All Saturday the gale continued, but though ice seemed to be brought up, out of sixteen vessels lying within short spaces of each other, all were more or less damaged, except the *Cumbrian* of Hull, and a Dutch vessel"(40).

The next day the middle fleet experienced the fury of the elements. One vessel, the *William and Anne* of Whitby, became a complete wreck and her master Captain William Terry, her carpenter and twelve seamen went on board the *Eagle* of Hull which was battling for survival. The log kept by Captain Matthew Wright, master of the *Eagle*, continues the story which began at 6 p.m. on 26th June:

" …a heavy press of loose floes broke up the dock and all hands were sawing ice and using every means to save the ship, she being lifted five feet out of the water forward. Our people working all night sawing ice around the ship, and working both pumps at times as she was making much water."

Five days were to pass before he could report that the assistance of two hundred or so men from neighbouring ships made it possible to "hove the ship up with her keel out forward", repair her, and heave her upright again (41).

On 1st July the most southerly ships were hit with great fury. The previous day Laing reported that the weather was alternately thick and clear, and that twenty five sail were in sight when the *Zephyr* made fast to a land floe in the evening. The next day the gale struck bringing with it "thick snowy weather". On 2nd July he paused to "contemplate the working of Divine Providence" when an opening in the ice enabled Captain Ash to locate the *Zephyr* in a less vulnerable situation away from "the weather side of the floe …The tempest raged all day with unabated fury," and "in a short span of time" Laing was to witness the sight of "four (i.e. five) vessels reduced to mere wrecks".

His sketches add a second dimension to his description of the "aweful and striking" scene but deep poignancy lies in an unnamed master's thoughts as he watched his ship sink beneath the ice, expressed in a letter written from Exeter Bay, Baffin Island on 5th September:

"On the 2nd of July our vessel, along with four others, was caught by the ice, which came with such overwhelming force against her, that it fairly lifted her out of the water, on the surface of the ice, as if to give us the last look of her, before she parted. She made a most majestic appearance, standing as upright as if she had been docked. It was not before the water had reached the cabin sole that I abandoned her, to take my seat on my chest that was standing on the ice, there to witness the last struggle of our gallant bark. I am unable to depict the magnificent scene that presented itself to my view; but it is one which would have suited either poet or painter. The first symptoms of destruction appeared among the half-deck planks; then the standing rigging and stays became slackened and nothing was heard but the crashing of the hull as she went to pieces. Her masts meantime slowly bent towards each other, as if to take their final adieu; and when they came in collision, they seemed to say, 'and must we part?' They then fell with a tremendous crash, and the hull was buried forever beneath a floe of ice six feet in thickness"(42).

By this time as many as a thousand seamen were living on the ice in Melville Bay in tents or underneath whaleboats. During the long hours of daylight northwards and southwards, flames and smoke from wrecked ships, torched once everything salvageable had been removed, signalled the extent of the devastation, and must have compounded the atmosphere of peril and isolation. Free from shipboard discipline, many found relief in the casks of salvaged rum, and scenes of gay festivity as the men ran loose on the ice were such that the experience came to be remembered as Baffin Fair. And yet no more than ten men lost their lives as a result of the catastrophe. Alexander Kidd of the *Achilles*, lost on 24th June, describes how he and so many others were brought home safely on the surviving ships:

"The crews remained by the vessels in the hope of saving their provisions and clothes; but this was found to be impracticable, and, as a last resort, the *Achilles* and the *Ville de Dieppe* were set fire to. In consequence of this, the after part of the hold of the French vessel, which contained the provisions, was entered and a considerable quantity of bread, beef, pork, brandy and wine was secured. The crews of the *Achilles* and the French ship were taken on board the *St. Andrew* of Aberdeen, and kindly treated. The number of hands on board of the *St. Andrew* now amounted to one hundred and fifty, and as the provisions were insufficient for so many, the majority of the shipwrecked crews resolved to proceed to some vessels which were perceived about twelve miles distant. Provisions were served out to them, and what clothes they had saved were put into the boats, which were dragged along the ice. The journey occupied about sixteen or seventeen days: during which the seamen were subjected to great privations by the inclemency of the weather; and some of the boats were destroyed which contained the few articles they had previously saved. On the 13th or 14th of July, they reached their destination, and were kindly and hospitably received by Captain Stevenson, of the *Horn*. There were at one time nine boats' crews on board of that vessel, but a number of them were afterwards transferred to others" (43).

Meanwhile Captain Ash had the opportunity to avail himself of the fruits of salvage from the *William* of Hull, wrecked just fifty yards from docks sheltering the *Zephyr* and the *Traveller* of Peterhead. The crews of both ships laboured for forty eight hours clearing field ice covering the sunken ship which rose out of the water. The upper part of the vessel was then fired in order to salvage casks of blubber stored below, but the right of the *Zephyr*'s crew to any they could recover was refused by Captain Ash. His cautious approach was later vindicated, when the claim of the master of the *Traveller* to the material he salvaged was decided in favour of the owners of the *William*, Messrs. Cooper of Hull, in an important case tried in the Admiralty Court in 1833 (44).

The two ships lay beset in the ice for two weeks, but Laing has no comment on the episode or of any assistance the *Zephyr*'s crew may have given towards restoring to seaworthiness the *Traveller*, which had been stove in the gale. On 17th July Captain Ash headed north and west in search of fish, but within a week it became obvious that there was little prospect of a passage to the "north waters", and the *Zephyr* lost no time in "endeavouring for a South passage". A month later they were abreast of Cape McCulloch (Pond's Inlet) on Baffin Island on the Canadian side of Baffin Bay. On 17th August Laing was able to join an expedition of six boats sent up an inlet in the area (perhaps into Eclipse Sound) on a fruitless search for whales.

Laing's sketches of ships and shipmates enclosed by moving ice at the mercy of the elements, convey a very strong impression of the peril and devastation of their recent experience. Now, with equal clarity, he expresses the relief which he and his companions must have felt as they stepped out of their boat on to "a fine sandy beach" to rest for a brief interlude. Feelings of relative safety, acute awareness and appreciation of his surroundings are implicit in his description of the "natural scenery of this dreary country". But it is in the "traces of some natives who had rested sometime before, also of deer and hare ...[and of] a few varieties of plants, the tints of some of which would not have dishonoured an European garden" that they found refreshment as they absorbed something of the natural and familiar. In the event it was a wild honey bee found by one of the men that brought "the recollection of our own favoured climate" most strongly to mind. Laing is moved to comment that "the Great Disposer of events has without doubt amply provided for their comfortable subsistence" in such inclement conditions.

The *Zephyr* moved steadily south, and on 18th September her "people [were] working at coiling the whale lines homeward bound". In this season of danger and disaster, experience, caution and a good measure of luck enabled Captain Ash to bring his ship safely home to Hull with some return to his owners stowed in her hold, harvested from just five whales secured in the Southwest fishing grounds off Baffin Island during May.

George Laing had left the *Zephyr* at Aberdeen on 15th October, almost a week after Captain Edward Dannatt of the *Progress* of Hull, wrecked on the afternoon of 2nd July, arrived at his home port with news of the disaster. By making long dangerous journeys across the ice from ship to ship he had reached England on 9th October aboard the *Abram*, the first ship home. His news brought great consternation to the people of Hull, and the price of oil rushed up to £60 a ton. There was great distress in the town that winter, the full measure of which was revealed at a meeting held at the Guildhall on 20th December when the Mayor opened a subscription for the support of Greenland whalers and their families (45).

14. A bottlenose whale and a caricature, possibly of Laing himself.

15. The **Jane**, **Viewforth** and **Middleton** beset in the Arctic in 1835; the **Jane** of Hull in the centre. Painted by Thomas Binks of Hull in 1836. (Hull Maritime Museum)

4. VOYAGE OF THE VOLUNTEER 1831

George Laing spent his second season in Arctic waters on an older and very well known whaler. The *Volunteer*, of 305 tons burden, laid down in Whitby in 1756, had made her first voyage to the Arctic in 1772. She was strengthened over the years and rebuilt in 1812 and returned to her home port with many good harvests, until her sale to Hull owners in 1825 reduced the Whitby fleet to just five vessels. Captain Henry Parrish, her master from 1831 to 1834, shared ownership with Thomas Harrison Marshall and Richard Marshall of Sculcoates, members of a family prominent in the Hull whaling industry. She was lost in 1843 (46).

The *Volunteer* set sail on 7th April 1831. George Laing carried his journal with him, and from the beginning there is a more positive note to his *Remarks* that is lacking in his record of his first season. He makes the most of a week's sojourn at Stromness in the Orkneys. A few months earlier the people of the busy little port had been the first to share the agony of whalemen returning home after enduring the fury of the Arctic. Now, while the complement of the *Volunteer* was completed and stores replenished and loaded before heading out for another season, the young surgeon had leisure to wander in its one dirty and refuse strewn little street to gather impressions of the people and their way of life. There is disapproval in his observation that "the barley brew is fully in as great plenty as in any other part of the globe". On the other hand, in the bird and animal life and in a nearby "lough which abounds in trout", he found familiar reminders of home as, daydreaming a little, he reflects that "a person possessed of an income of £70 to £100 might pass his lifetime in comfort and peace". In reality, and by contrast, memories of the previous year's experience with the prospect of danger and privation ahead, must have lain heavily upon Laing.

Captain Parrish headed out from Stromness for the Arctic on 19th April and by 6th May the *Volunteer* had made the pack ice. Laing tracks the whaler's passage and reports the chain of information passed from ship to ship as the fleet made its way towards the far north. On 14th June they made fast to a small iceberg "about a gunshot from the southernmost of Buchans Three Isles" in Melville Bay at latitude 74^0N.

They were in company with about a "dozen more ships" described elsewhere by George Laing as "the grand fleet". One vessel harboured the surgeon of the *John* of Greenock, the last ship to founder in the previous year, who with other members of the crew had been forced to take refuge and winter over in Greenland at the Danish colony at Upernavik (called Opermweek by the whalers (47). The voyage of this vessel, the circumstances of its loss, and the fate of the crew is completely out of keeping with the experience of other ships and their crews lost in the storms of 1830. In most cases the more fortunate made every effort to succour the shipwrecked and willingly provided the manpower which enabled more than one stricken vessel to be restored to seaworthiness after sustaining crippling damage in the heaving, storm lashed Arctic pack ice.

The visit of the surgeon of the *John* to the *Volunteer* was of some significance to Laing, who carefully recounts the unusual circumstances surrounding the party's leaving the *John*. There had been difficulties in 1829, when the vessel had been engaged as a tender to the little three masted schooner *Victory* commanded by Captain John Ross, setting out on a voyage of exploration to thread through the islands north of Baffin Island in yet another search for a North West Passage. Before the expedition had left Scotland most of the crew of the *John* had mutinied and gone ashore, and Captain Ross was forced to sail for the Arctic without the tender. Yet in 1830 the same master, Captain Coombe, officers and crew headed out for the northern fishery in the whaler where, in Baffin Bay, her unruly crew seems to have mutinied again.

Whatever the circumstances, Captain Coombe had died before the surgeon, mate and a boat's crew left the ship "with the agreement of those aboard" to head for the Danish settlement. However, the ice opened up unexpectedly while the land party was still within hailing distance of the *John*, and they made all haste to rejoin their ship. George Laing was to make a point of stressing the fact that the surgeon had told him that the party were as close to the *John* as to be able to make out "the peculiar dress of an individual on the rigging", and yet their desperate signals expressing their wish to re-embark were ignored by those remaining on board. They found themselves abandoned as the *John* got underweigh in charge of the specksioneer (chief harpooner), carrying with her crew members from the wrecked *Princess of Wales* and of the *Laetitia*. Her charts and log-glasses had been taken ashore by the mate, and for about a week the *John* was navigated cautiously during daylight hours only. The resumption of night sailing was her downfall when on 24th September the watch on deck sighted a line of breakers which he mistook for a stream of ice and the teak-built vessel was wrecked on the coast of Baffin Island. The crew were brought home by the *Swan* and the *Duncombe* of Hull (48).

Another vessel in "the grand fleet" at the time was the *Hercules* of Aberdeen, whose surgeon kept a journal notable for its description of the varied and beautiful bird life of the Arctic, and for the number the unidentified writer was able to slaughter with his "double percussion fowling piece" (49). He also took every opportunity to observe and learn about Inuit, known to whalemen as "Yaks". Laing reveals his interest in these people when he records a visit to the *Zephyr* by two men hoping to barter a "few sea horses [walrus] tusks and two sealskins". He describes their physical characteristics and notes that they eagerly traded their "outer dress" for "knives and sharp-edged tools" (50).

A number of Inuit were moving between the ships at Buchans (ie. Baffins) Three Isles in 1831 but Laing has no comment. The surgeon of the *Hercules* made the most of the contact and records his first impressions:

"One of them entered our cabin. He was a little stout made fellow about 5 feet 5 inches high about 22 years of age of a clear olive brown complexion with long coarse black hair hanging about his ears his face was broad and his cheeks blown up with fat like blubber. He had on a white sort of cotton jerkin with sealskin skirts sealskin breeches and boots with a white seal cap on his head. He offered a sealskin jerkin for sale I offered him a pair of cloth trowsers for his jerkin which after a minute inspection he took. He had white whale's teeth for buttons on his jerkin. The old yacks had dark mahogany complexions, their eyes were placed far apart" (51).

About five hundred Inuit had spent the previous winter in the vicinity of Upernavik, and the surgeon of the *Hercules* sought the company of the surgeon of the *John* to learn all he could about life among them. The former's interest provides the reader with a picture of a winter spent under the protection of these people, as he records the experiences of the surgeon of the *John* who described:

" ...the manners of the Eskimaux to each other as most admirable in all the relations of life. During all the seven months that he spent among them he never saw a son refuse to obey his father's bidding ...They are very hospitable and gave the wrecked seamen a share of what they had. The winter was a very hard one for the sealing as the continued gales of South west wind never suffered the bay ice to form. The Eskimaux at a settlement about 50 miles from Opermwick were obliged to eat the leather off their canoes and that of their boots and had it not been for some assistance afforded them by the Danes they must all have perished ...(52). The Eskimaux are a shortlived people ... infants are quite fair at their birth."

The surgeon of the *John* spoke of Inuit hunting methods;
"noting that they feared ... no animal but the sea-horse (walrus) which sometimes sinks their canoes with his tremendous tusks, however they kill considerable numbers of them ... He described their practice of setting dogs upon a bear ...to distract his attention (when) he rises on end the esquimaux whistles off his dogs and shoots the bear with his rifle ...He once saw a boy of 10 years of age kill an old bear and two cubs with his father's rifle, his father being asleep."

Whalemen were always on the alert for the great white predators, and encounters with them have their place in most accounts of whaling voyages. Laing's journal is no exception as he writes of a perilous encounter of his own making. The surgeon of the *Hercules* reports the measure of their danger to shipwrecked whalemen:

" ...the ship's company, when they had their chests and bedding on the ice were very much alarmed by the boldness of the bears which were very numerous and savage with hunger some of them tore open their chests and scattered their bedding about. One bear was seen to make a spring off the ice at a living whale which was lying close to the edge so that they were obliged to back off and were prevented for a short time from striking in a second harpoon."

This was the hair raising experience of the crew of the *James* of Peterhead, one of three ships lost in Melville Bay in June 1831.

*   *   *   *

John Laing's account of his Arctic experiences is filled out with observations and scientific data, in keeping with a great public interest in works dealing with travel and natural history at the time. The detailed nature of George Laing's account of a week spent at Stromness in 1831 before the *Volunteer* headed out for Arctic waters may suggest that, in his turn, he planned to expand and publish his private journal; indeed there is a strong family tradition that he proposed to do so. He could have chosen to record many experiences in the small green leather bound notebook he carried to the Arctic aboard two Hull whalers. But his *Remarks* trace their voyages, and his sketches, carefully naming stricken vessels, are graphic impressions of the devastation of the great storm of 1830. In that year he wrote up in great detail his treatment of Bourmaster Spence, and in doing so has left an interesting study for medical men today (53). In 1831 he has no comment on his care of crewmen he was called upon to treat, except to report the loss of "one of our Orkneymen pitched overboard from off the bowsprit every exertion being made proved in vain from the heavy swell".

The next day, 2nd October, Captain Parrish hoisted the *Volunteer*'s ensign to signal that she was homeward bound. Few whales had been sighted as the whaler, at the mercy of the elements, followed the coast of Greenland as far north as Cape York before turning south and west. She had weathered storms, and on at least one occasion was "expected to become a wreck" as her crew watched the hull of the *Neptune* of London disappear beneath the ice. More than once during the voyage the *Volunteer* was to meet with the *Lee* of Hull, whose master, Captain Lee, had been since 1825 the first to head out from Hull for northern waters; his boldness in venturing time and again into the ice without another ship in sight had rewarded him with the top harvest season after season. In 1831 he had slipped out of Hull a month earlier than Captain Parrish and, even though he was prevented by adverse weather from breaking into the summer feeding grounds north of Melville Bay, his tally of eleven whales making 175 tons of oil taken in south western waters off Baffin Island, again made the *Lee* the best fished of the Hull fleet. By contrast the *Volunteer* carried in her hold oil and whalebone harvested from just two whales, one captured early in the season in the vicinity of Disco Island off Greenland, and the other across Davis Strait near Cape Searle, just a week before heading for home, a lower return to her owners than that of the *Zephyr* the previous year.

Laing had abandoned his daily log when the *Volunteer* "bore up for home", but he materially fills out his account of the season's whaling in a draft report to some unnamed authority, most likely to be the ship's owners. He seems to be supporting the actions of the master and part-owner, Captain Parrish, when he expresses the strong opinion that nothing was to be gained from "proceeding early to the north [waters]", and expounds on the exigencies of the ice and its effect on various sections of the fleet. While ice bound at Baffins Three Islands he had been ashore and "in company with a number of the commanders" who, with "the aid of glasses and mature judgements", were very discouraged with the sight of "a solid sheet of ice interspersed with numberless Icebergs" as far as the eye could "reach." He notes that he witnessed the wreck of the *Neptune* of London in a tremendous gale from the south west, and reveals that he had reported the previous season's experiences on the *Zephyr*. There is particular reference to the situation which forced the surgeon of the ill-fated *John* of Greenock and his companions to winter over in Greenland, which suggests that Laing is obviously intent upon setting straight a record of events, which can only imply divergence between the story told him by the surgeon and the account given by survivors brought home a year earlier.

What lay behind this fragment remains to be discovered but George Laing had obviously learned much, and in years to come would pass on his memories to his sons. The small volume undoubtedly has its place in documenting the story of the whalemen who, year by year, shipped out of Hull on sturdy full-rigged vessels to battle and best the perils of the Arctic.

16. First of a series of drawings in the journal of the **Volunteer***, 1831.*

17. The **Gilder** *and* **North Briton** *(identified by inscription bottom right); compare with Gibson drawing (pl. 13) numbers 1 and 2.*

5. THE JOURNAL AND A
CONTEMPORARY DRAWING

The accounts of the two voyages are written in a small pocket book of forty two leaves (7 $^3/_4$ x 6 $^1/_2$ in.) with green leather covers. One or two sketches, the most detailed, were removed from the journal early last century and were destroyed in a house fire in 1934. The contents must clearly have been shown to Edward Gibson (1787 – 1859), a local shipbuilder and promoter of the arts. He assembled several of the sketches of the vessels beset in the 1830 season into a single watercolour drawing now preserved in Hull Trinity House, by whose permission it is here reproduced.

Gibson was a judge of the first two exhibitions, 1827 and 1829, of the Hull and East Riding Institution for the Promotion of the Fine Arts, but his interest in the events of 1830 were more practical than artistic. He was a shareholder in the *North Briton*, owning eight sixty-fourths, a significant financial investment. The drawing is evidently an attempt to record and understand the events which led to the loss of the *North Briton* and other vessels in the fleet.

The drawing is entitled 'A sketch of the position of some of the vessels at the late perilous fishery, laying in Baffin Bay, Lat. 72^0 14'N, land twenty five miles E. DAVIS STRAITS.' The individual ships are numbered and identified by a key: 1 and 2 (far left) *North Briton* of Hull, *Gilder* do. Lost; 3 *Alexander*, Aberdeen; 4 *Three Brothers*, Dundee; 5 *William* do. Lost; 6 *Traveller* of Peterhead; 7 (in the foreground) *Zephyr* of Hull. Signed E. Gibson 1830 bottom right. The whole measures 12$^1/_4$ x 15$^1/_4$ ins. [See pl.13]

Regrettably there are no representations of the *Zephyr* other than the Gibson and Laing sketches and no pictures of the *Volunteer* of any quality. The collection of marine paintings in the Hull Maritime Museum is outstanding, but it so happens that the two which show the *Volunteer* are among the poorest and are not even an adequate representation of a whaleship as a type, let alone as a portrait of a particular vessel!

The sketches made by Laing were made towards the back of the pocket book, and though depicting events in 1830, are sandwiched between the end of the 1831 text and the description of the medical treatment of Bourmaster Spence. Elsewhere in this volume are additional illustrations selected as images of Tayport, Hull and the Arctic fishery, including the work of George Laing's son, Francis.

It may be noted that both in 1830 and 1831 Laing begins his journal with the briefest of descriptions of the departure from Hull, followed by a short account of his time in Shetland aboard the *Zephyr*, and Orkney in the *Volunteer*.

There is then a gap and the entries begin again on 6th May when the vessels reach Greenland. There is no mention of the traditional May Day ceremony when Neptune and his minions initiated the 'greenhands' who had never visited the Arctic before, and the garland was hoisted. The garland was bedecked with ribbons and tokens from the whalers' wives and sweethearts. The somewhat puritanical Laing may have disapproved of these celebrations when discipline was relaxed, and especially as it was usual for rum or other spirits to be available. A bottle of whisky (or some tea, sugar etc.) was often given to Neptune as a means of propitiation to ensure that the victim was treated gently by the barber and his helpers, otherwise one could be heavily lathered, cruelly scraped with a hoop iron razor and drenched in water.

The text of the journal is published here as written except for additional punctuation and division into manageable sentences.

Front end paper; rough sketch of whale and opposite a sketch of a bottle nose whale and of a fantastical male figure. The costume seems to be part Eskimo combined with moustache, beard and strange head-dress. Possibly this is a self-caricature of Laing himself dressed in Eskimo clothing and Scottish tam o' shanter. [Pl.14]

The name of Newburgh where George Laing was born appears twice, also a list of names and stores; H. Randal F.N. Tronson (?) Trouser (?)

1lb coffee, 4lb sugar, M. Hilton 1lb coffee – 2lb sugar

another ….the … …does blame

love the Earl (?) Case (?)

them a speedy passage comes

and night into the south

where the whale fish blow

Overleaf is inscribed: -

Diary of my Father Dr. George Laing

Rebound by David S. Laing 31st July 1911

28th Sept 1831 Cape Searle

11 Drawers

11 Singlets

4 Stockings

4 Shirts

Then follow the journal entries beginning on the facing page.

6. A FEW REMARKS ON A VOYAGE FROM HULL TO DAVIS STRAITS IN THE SHIP *ZEPHYR* CAPTAIN ROBERT ASH 1830

On Wednesday morning, the 24th March, sailed from Hull with a fresh breeze from the westward at 9 a.m. rounded the Spurn light and made all sail towards Lerwick the principal town of the Shetland Islands. On Saturday the 27th in the morning got moored in the harbour where we found about twenty sail lying wind bound principally on our passage from Hull to Lerwick. We had for the most part clear weather with fresh breezes from the westward.

May 6th. This morning we made the south west. Ice in latitude 62⁰ North long. 58⁰ 22' West with a strong breeze from the N.N.E. accompanied with severe frost. We had been five weeks on our passage from Shetland during which period we had for the most part boisterous weather, with the winds predominating from the north and westward. On the 18th April we passed an Iceberg. On the 25th Cape Farewell bore E.S.E. distance forty miles. On approaching the land we were almost everyday boarded by small land birds, although some times at the distance of four or five hundred miles they were seldom absent. On our passage across we were also generally in sight of some of the other whalers proceeding in the same direction.

May 12th. The pack ice seemed very irregular and but ill adapted for the fishery. The off ice however lay in fine detached streams and pieces, and appeared well fitted for that purpose: they were however only to be seen close along the edge of the former. Wind still from the northward and ship continues plying to windward among loose pieces and streams of ice. Yesterday killed a bottle nose.

June 1st. Since last date the winds have prevailed from the south and eastward with changeable weather from the change of wind. The ice packed together, we struck six whales and secured four. The loss of the two was owing to the lines breaking. Several ships in coy – lat. 63⁰.

June 20th. Since last date the winds have prevailed from the north east and eastward with some light breezes from the south accompanied with a good deal of hazey (sic) weather. On the 3rd killed a small whale measuring 6' 6" in bone and filling only 8 butts blubber. Ship making all possible sail to the north today plying along the land abreast of Black Hook, with a breeze from the north with hazey (sic) weather. The late prevalence of easterly winds seemed to have packed the ice off to the westward.

June 20th. So that our oldest fishermen never remember of having seen such a body of water, so far, at this time of the season. Lat. 71⁰ 15' North.

June 26th. This evening made the ship fast to the land floe, the Devil's

Thumb bearing about S.E. by S. distance fifteen or twenty miles, *William* of Hull, *Phoenix* of Whitby, *Egginton* of Kirk[c]aldy and *Neptune* of Aberdeen in company: on the 21st a fine southerly breeze sprung up which continued until now, although this evening it augmented to (?) violence and closed the ice so that we could go no farther.

June 30th. Since last date have been employed in towing and tracking ship to the northward along the land floe. Weather alternately thick and clear. Twenty five sail in sight at night, made fast to the land floe.

July 10th. On the first of the month it came to blow a strong gale from the S.W. accompanied with thick snowy weather; this prevented our further progress to the northward. On the 2nd the gale continued with unabated vigor (sic) which made us all tremble for our safety: our ship being laid along the weather side of the floe and exposed to the press of the ice from the southward, but here I must pause and contemplate the working of Divine Providence. This morning did the ice open a little and allow us to haul our ship under the lee of the point where, had we laid as at first, we certainly stood a great chance of being wrecked and, deplorable to relate, placed in this same situation did we witness ere long sufficient proofs: having called all hands to make a dock, we put our ship into it, and ere this attempt for our safety was half accomplished we observed the *William* of Hull had hoisted a signal [of] great distress; a few hours after followed by another from the *Three Brothers* of Dundee. By this time "the Fine Ship *William*" had become a total wreck; the tempest raged the whole day with unabated fury. In the afternoon signals of distress were seen from three other ships viz. the *Alexander* of Dundee with the *Gilder* and *North Briton* of Hull, and in a short span of time these aforesaid four vessels were reduced to mere wrecks.

The scene was aweful (sic) and striking to behold. When the last and most fatal press came on, masts were to be seen buckling and bending, and the ships heaved and tossed like as if they had been in the troubled ocean. What added greatly to the wretchedness of the spectacle were intoxicated sailors sauntering too and froe (sic) upon the ice together with hundreds of poor fellows destitute of a habitation or a covering for themselves in this dreary and inclement country. Happy am I to add however that this was obtained for them in the ships that were yet spared. On the 4th three men crossed the ice from a fleet of ships about twelve miles northward and added to the list of destruction, they reported the loss of the *Laurel* of Hull, *Resolution* of Peterhead, *Hope* of Peterhead, *Princess of Wales* of Aberdeen, *Letitia* of Aberdeen; *Middleton* of Aberdeen and *William and Anne* of Whitby together with some others severely damaged with the ice. I also received a letter from David [his elder brother] sent along with my chest in the *Volunteer* of Hull. On the 7th the gale abated. We lay beset, in company with the *Traveller* of Peterhead untill (sic) the 17th when we cast off and proceeded to the N.W. on the 25th. We fell in with the *Juno* of Leith, *Union* of Peterhead and *Hercules* of Aberdeen. From their commanders we had the opinion of the little probability of a North passage being obtained for a considerable time which, combined with our own idea, determined us to loose (sic) no time in endeavouring for a south passage. In the mean time being favoured with a fresh breeze from the northward we run south with all possible sail set. On the 26th, after a good deal of trouble and perseverance, we got in to the south water in latitude 73⁰ 40' – 22 sail in compy. On the 31st we were in latitude 71⁰ 34' when we took the ice, there being some probability of getting to the westward in the evening, were obliged to make fast, could get no further.

August. On the afternoon of the 1st August the prospect of procuring a passage to the westward was very discouraging, and the season now rapidly drawing to a close determined us to endeavour to get further to the south, where the chance of getting to the westward was greater. On the 9th August our latitude was 70⁰ 42'; for nearly two days previous the weather has been thick and foggy with a strong breeze from the S.W. We were therefore prevented from a[s]certaining the state of the ice, and as a person often goes a wrong road in a dark night, we did not attempt to proceed to the westward.

August 9th. This morning it cleared away, and our expectations being to all appearance realized their being no stoppage, we therefore made all sail and run to the westward on the afternoon. The long wished for sight appeared the west land of Davis Straits about forty miles distant. At eight in the evening we reached the land ice, and there in former times the anxious fisherman was almost sure to compleat (sic) his voyage, but to accomplish this we now saw no probability, having still a strong breeze from the S.W. we run to northward along the land ice. On the 11th we were nearly abreast of Cape McCulloch in lat. 71⁰ 34' and had only seen two straggling fish since we made the land ice on the August 11th. A strange sail in sight next morning, there being no appearance of land ice to the northward we stood off to the eastward. Early the next morning reached the middle ice; ere night we had seen three fish but could not get hold of one, they were all making to the N.E. Two sail in sight, again made towards the land which we reached on the 15th. Sent six boats in shore in search of fish but they returned unsuccessful. On the 17th again sent six boats up an inlet in one of which I myself went, here the natural scenery of this dreary country struck me with admiration and wonder. Stupendous rocks rising from two to three hundred feet with flat perpendicular surfaces above the level of the water, more inland lofty mountains whose various formed summits were clad with eternal snow and capt (sic) with the clouds which generally are present; we rowed up the inlet until we came to fine sandy beach where we landed. The land here formed a fine level valley bounded on the east and west by high perpendicular rocks and terminating by a gradual a[s]cent to the northward, except in one place which led to the eastward round the back of the high land that towards the shore formed the steep margin on the northern side of the inlet. Here we found traces of some natives who had rested some time before, also of deer and hares, although we did not see any. The scanty soil afforded subsistence to a few varieties of plants, the tints of some of which would not have dishonoured an European garden, but here I am inclined to think that flowers like many other things are not to be estimated by their brilliant appearance. A wild honey bee found by one of the men more strongly brought the recollection of our own favor'd climate to my mind – that these insects propagate the species in this desolate country must, I think, be a natural conclusion, but here surely "the beacon of industry" can have only a short time to provide for his winter subsistence.* Three months there is at most of any thing like summer weather in general, one half of which is made up of thick, raining and stormy weather; but that Great Disposer of events has without doubt amply provided for their comfortable subsistence. Indeed I, a short sighted and ignorant mortal might have my eyes opened by a research into the labours of the naturalist who have now-adays gone so far to clear our minds upon these subjects. Having rested here for some time and refreshed, we rowed to the other side of the inlet which at this place was about four miles broad. Nothing occurred worthy of remark, only that we saw a whale on our passage and which we gave unsuccessful chase to. The day being now far spent, we made all haste to get on board of the ship which we reached about 9 o'clock. We had nearly lost our way, a thick fogg (sic) having come on an hour before, and only found our way by the report of a musket fired on board of the ship we had spoken, the *Eclipse* of Peterhead, the day before who gave us the account of the loss of the *Spencer* of Montrose.

* A state of torpor must be the state they remain in in Winter.

     <u>August 24th</u>. With a few intervals since the 17th, the weather had been thick and foggy with the winds predominating from the southward. Ship making all sail to the south, on the 22nd made fast to a berg one and a half miles from the land here in the evening.

     <u>August 22nd</u>. We were visited by two of the natives in canoes. They had got sight of the ship in the middle part of the day it being then clear, but at this time it was very thick and had been so for some hours previous, so that I think without signals being given, our situation could alone have been found out by those enured (sic) to the changeableness and variety of this dreary climate. The sun appeared to be their reference and guide, but even this great reviver of nature is scarcely to be distinguished in thick foggy weather. They came on board with all the familiarity immaginable (sic), shouting the words "chymo" "pilley day" "Jackreny" etc. They stood about 5ft. 4 inches in height, long black hair of a copper colour with remarkable neat hands and feet, and very active and quick in their motions. They manifested a good deal of surprise and curiosity at the different articles on board. They seemed at first rather unwilling to leave their canoes, and at last, when we had so far gained their confidence which we deserved,

     <u>August 22nd</u>. they mentioned the words "no tittlepoop" meaning not to steal anything. All the barter they brought on board was a few sea horses tusks and two seals' skins – but our people did not like to be altogether disappointed in this, so that they were induced and with great goodwill exchanged their outer dress for knives and sharp edged tools which they most eagerly sought after. As a supply in case of being overtaken by hunger they brough[t] along with them a piece of putrid seal's flesh, a most disgusting repast to a civilized people.

     <u>August 24th</u>. A strong breeze from the N. E. Ship dodging and plying to windward. At noon cleared up, spoke to the *Madamoiselle* – Captain Guedon who gave us the account of the loss of the *Oxenhope* and the *Progress* of Hull –

Baffin and the *Rattler* of Leith – *Achilles* of Dundee and a French vessel the *Ville de Dieppe* – Captn. Masse, also the death of Captn. North which happened on the 26th July. This unfortunate man, at the time of his ship being wrecked, exposed himself for nearly a whole day upon the ice, which, together with grief and disapointment (sic) I believe brought him to a premature end. Since the 24th have had almost incessant thick weather.

September 1st. Ship making all way to the southward. On the 26th fell in with straggling ice. On the 27th spoke the *Fairy* of Dundee who had come from the south, Captn. Welch mentioned that there was no ice with a heavy swell so that there was very little probability of doing any good. 28th spoke the *Keiro* and the *Brunswick* of Hull lat. 68⁰ 30' N.

September 1st. Today cleared up, stood in with the land. Saw two fish in the afternoon. Spoke the *Grenville Bay* of Newcastle in the evening; run to the northward, *Fairy* in company.

September 7th. Since the 1st have had cloudy weather with intervals of clear. On the 5th , lat. 71⁰ 14' spoke the *Caledonia* of Kircaldy (sic) who has come from lat. 72⁰. Stood in for the land. Today in sight distance twenty miles; no fish seen.

September 10th. Since the 7th have been making all sail to the southward. This morning reached in with the land, Brodie Bay, in lat. 68⁰ 16' N; weather thick and hazey (sic), *Wm. Torr* and *Keiro* (sic) in compy.

September 17th. Since last date ship dodging and plying along the land; no fish seen. Weather for the most part clear and fine. Today a strong breeze from the N.E; in the evening distance from the land half a mile. We had a narrow escape from being driven ashore, the swell being direct upon it and the wind having fallen, but that Watchful Providence who had hitherto preserved us, sent a breeze to our relief; hazey (sic) weather.

September 18th. Strong breeze from the N.E. with thick hazey (sic) weather distance from the land about twenty five miles. In the afternoon spoke the *Andrew Marvel* (sic) of Hull who had only got clear of the ice in Melville Bay on the 7th ulto. They left a considerable number of ships there beset. Ship running S.W. by S.; people working a[t] coiling the whale lines. Homeward bound.

Landed at Aberdeen 15th October.

7. REMARKS ON A VOYAGE TO DAVIS STRAITS IN THE SHIP *VOLUNTEER*, HENRY PARISH COMMANDER

Mustered hands on the 5th April 1831. Set sail on the forenoon of the 7th and plyed down the Humber; on the afternoon of the 8th rounded Spurn lights. Fresh breezes from the southward. Weather hazy with showers.

April 11th. Today arrived at Stromness harbour after a fine run from the Humber of seventy two hours during which the winds prevailed from the S.E. On the evening of the 10th saw Buchanness and Kinardshire. At 7 o'clock on the morning of the 11th took a pilot on board from Wick; the two preceding days hazy with showers.

Tuesday 19th. Early this morning a breeze sprung up form the S.S.E. with which we got underweigh to proceed on our voyage. Since we had come to anchor at Stromness the weather was for the most part clear and comparatively fine. I had many opportunities of going on shore. The country here cannot be called mountainous, the prospect generally being that of gently sloping land. The only high land observed here are two high hills on the north west corner of Hoy Island. The inhabitants are evidently a little more refined than their brethren of the Shetland Islands. A considerable number of the female part are employed in plaiting leghorn for London Merchants - farming is in a more improved state than in the Shetland, ploughs, carts etc. being more plentiful; the breed of cattle and horses appear also to be larger. I was told that their [sic] are gardens in this quarter that could compete with nearly any in Briton [sic]. Wild fowl are plentiful; those I observed were black shags, kittiweaks [sic], of variously marked ducks chiefly black with white breasts and spots of white, intermixed with the black large gulls etc, etc. The first morning that I went on shore I was quite enchanted with the melodious tunes of numerous larks warbling in the air. Plenty of grouse and rabbits are found, hares have lately been introduced; badgers are also wild here.

The town consists, principally, of a single street, if such it can be called, for in walking along it almost at every step you are obliged to make angles both acute and obtuse, saluted at every corner with a wiff of peat reck [reek] to arouse you to behold the miserable mass of confusion around you. Almost upon every sign board you observe that the barley brew [brec?] is fully in as great plenty here as in any other quarter of the globe. The designations appeared generally odd to me, such as "Bakie Goudie" Licenced etc. The places of public worship consist of an established church and a dissenting meeting house. Public amusements are rare amongst the inhabitants. I fancy the same notion prevails as in Kirkwall, namely that to dance is contrary to the dictates of religion. Here they have a billiard table where those who can afford occasionally spend their time. Its situation is not very attractive being placed in a solitary garret. About a mile distant from the town their [sic] is a lough which abounds in trout. Indeed I think that were a person possessed of an income of from £70 to £100 a year, that he might pass his lifetime in comfort and peace. On proceeding out of Hoy, I observed that the west side of the islands were bounded by steep rocks. Indeed a person might, a priori, been led to expect so from its exposed situation, especially, the action of the waters of the western deep seem to have made visible ravages, some huge masses of rock being quite detached apparently, from the mainland. One part in particular is remarkable, a little distance to the south of the sound, and is called "The Old man of Hoy".

May 6th. Today made the pack ice in lat. 60⁰ long. 59'W. Yesterday the *Swan* of Hull passed us, plying to windward, wind at east, a strong breeze. Have had an excellent passage from Stromness of sixteen days duration; the winds during our run prevailed for the S.E. to N.E. We found the pack ice in a [sic].

Saturday 7th. Fine clear weather. Wind E.N.E., ship plying to windward along the pack ice; people employed in getting the boats out and the lines coiled. Lat. 60⁰ 50'N long. 61⁰ 53'W.

Sunday. Fine clear weather, fresh breezes as before. Ship plying to windward.

Monday 9th. Weather fine and clear. Light airs and calms lat. 60⁰ 43'N.

Tuesday 10th. Thick snowy weather. Winds E.S.E. strong breezes. Ship plying to the north among streams of ice; at noon several sail in company. Lat.-

Wednesday 11th. Light winds and thick hazey [sic] weather with a heavy swell. Ship plying to windward lat. 61⁰ 56'.

Thursday. Fine clear weather, wind W.N.W., a number of ships in coy, spoke the *Isabella* of Hull. Ship dodging and running to the northward along the pack edge. Today got into dark coloured water.

Friday. Ditto winds and weather. Ship dodging and running to the northward, a number of ships in coy. Lat 62⁰ 46'N.

Saturday. Winds and weather much the same. Ship plying to windward among the ice. No fish seen, yet we had some days before heard of some whales having been caught lat. 63⁰ 22'N.

Sunday 15th. Fine clear weather. Ship plying and dodging among streams of ice. Saw a fish and sent four boats away; not successful however.

Monday 16th. Weather fine, fresh breeze from the N. by E., ship as before. Saw the *Lee* of Hull secure their fifth fish, a number of ships in coy. Lat. 63⁰ 40'N.

Tuesday and Wednesday. Weather fine and clear, ship plying and running among the ice. Winds variable lat. 63⁰ 35'.

Thursday. Wind N.E. This afternoon run out of the ice to proceed to the northward.

Sunday 22nd. Variable breezes from the northward with clear weather. Ship plying to the windward along the ice. Lat. 64⁰ 40' North.

Monday 23rd. Wind east. Ship running to the northward. Caught some small land birds.

<u>Tuesday 24th and Wednesday 25th</u>. Weather for the most part clear. Ship running to the northward. The land in sight lat. 68⁰ North. Several ships in sight, broken up ice lay about thirty miles to the westward of the land in this latitude.

<u>Thursday 26th and Friday 27th</u>. Thick foggs [sic]. Wind at S.W., ship dodging at the edge of the ice about sixty miles to the westward of Disco Island.

<u>Saturday 28th</u>. Early this morning the wind veered to the N.E. In the afternoon the fog cleared away, when we made all sail and plyed to the north along the ice. Two ships in sight.

<u>Sunday 29th</u>. Winds etc. etc. Ditto.

<u>Monday 30th</u>. Ditto. In the forenoon picked up a dead whale which measured 11ft 4in. in bone. It had been struck by the *Swan* of Hull and had suffered no deterioration when we found it.

<u>Tuesday 31st</u>. Fresh breezes at E.N.E. Ship plying to westward under double reefed topsails, people employed in making off the blubber which amounts to fifty eight butts. Several ships passed us making all sail to the northward.

<u>Wednesday June 1st</u> - <u>Thursday 2nd and Friday the 3rd</u>. Strong breezes at E.N.E. Ship plying along the ice. On the 2nd saw a ship with a whale in tow.

<u>Saturday 4th</u> Winds southerly strong breezes. Ship running along the ice to the northward. Saw a fish sent two boats after. Passed the *Dorothy* fast to a whale which they lost lat. 70⁰ 40'.

<u>Sunday 5th</u>. Ship making all sail to the north with winds as before and clear weather.

<u>Monday 6th</u>. Fine clear weather. Light variable airs, about forty sail in company and in sight. Heard the sad intelligence of the loss of the *James*, Capt. Hogg of Peterhead near Black Hook during the N.E. gales that had prevailed on the previous week. The whales had been uncomonly [sic] numerous in that latitude about the time the unfortunate vessel was wrecked, and we understand had three of them on board when she perished.

We also learned that the men that had quited [sic] the *John* of Greenock when beset in Melville Bay last year, had ultimately reached Opermweek, a southern Danish settlement, although their sufferings had been great. We learned that one of them has lost both legs from the effects of exposure. Today ship dodging about twenty miles to the westward of the land. Lat. 73⁰ 48'N.

<u>Saturday 11th June</u>. Ship made fast to the land ice [8 miles to the north westward of - this section crossed out] Duck Islands bearing S.W. along with about a dozen more ships. Weather fine, with the wind from the W.S.W. Moderate breeze yesterday took the ice, for several days previous had been dodging about in the clear water. Ice seems a good deal broke up to the northward, with immense number of icebergs.

<u>Tuesday 14th</u>. Weather thick with a moderate breeze from the N.E. by E. - ship made fast to a small iceberg about a gunshot from the southern most of Buchans [ie. Baffins] Three Isles. On Sunday the 12th we had fine clear weather with light southerly airs. Early on Monday morning got underweigh and tracked ship to the southward again. The water getting less around us and every appearance of a southerly breeze. About four hours after made fast to a floe,

could get no further, a single bar only intervening between us and the south water. On Tuesday got through and made for our present situation. Today had a visit from the surgeon of the *John* of Greenock, which vessel perished at this country last year. He mentioned that they had left the ship in lat. 76^0 40' with the intention of proceeding towards a Danish colony. On the 16th September the surgeon, together with the mate and some of the crew, parted from the ship on the undertaking with the agreement of the rest of the ship's company. A few hours after leaving, and while yet at the distance of two miles from the vessel, a prospect appeared of the ship being able to be got extricated from the ice, when they, viz the boat's crew, made signals that they intended to return again and join the ship - the people on board, however gave no heed to them, but made all expedition and got underweigh, and notwithstanding the exertions of the boats crew to overtake them they got out of their sight as the night fell. It is thought by the remaining survivors belonging to the boat that there was no excuse from those that were in the vessel (on the score) of not seeing their signals, as when they threw them out, the peculiar dress of an individual on board of the ship could even be distinguished.

In order to render the probability greater of reaching the ship, the boat had been lightened of provisions, cloths etc. which were placed upon the ice. At the time the surgeon and the mate had left the boat to plant the signals up on a hummock of ice for the purpose of rendering them conspicuous. Five of their crew with the sensuality of brutes got quite stupified with liquor. On their return, after concluding their unsuccessful pursuit, their next care was to endeavour to find their provisions which they left upon the ice and then to make all expedition to a Danish Colony; but for the present being so exhausted they intended resting a few hours and then continuing the search for their provisions. While settling this point, the five individuals who had besotted themselves although strongly entreated to the contrary by those who retained their sober senses, insisted upon going immediately to the search. The remainder of the boat's crew after a few hours of disturbed rest, next concerned how they should find their drunken comrades, provisions etc., explored all around but no trace could be descried. They hovered in the neighbourhood all day. In the evening their boat being in want of repair they hauled it up upon the ice which, when they had done so, they discovered the boat's jack, which had been previously placed as a mark for their provisions, with the appearance of objects moving to and fro immediately (on which – these two words erased) discovered, made haste and returned the signal and went to meet their ill-fated shipmates. But, whilst thus endeavouring to save them, they by some means lost sight alas never to see them more, and no doubt is entertained but that they met a watery grave. The poor survivors were now destitute of provisions. The next morning they picked up 30 lbs. of bread. After surprising hardships and fatigues they reached Opermwick eleven days after leaving their vessel.

Wednesday, Thursday and Friday. Weather thick with moderate winds from the N.E. Ship still made fast to the iceberg.

Saturday 18th. Light breezes from the south; cast off and plyed to the south.

Sunday 19th. Wind N.E.; weather alternately thick and clear. Ship plying north, about sixty five ships in sight. In the morning the *Zephyr* of Hull and some other ships run to the southward. At night we made fast to a floe, there being no possibility of getting further.

Saturday 25th. Since last date the weather has been for the most part thick and hazy accompanied with snow showers and cold; light variable winds. Ship sometimes made fast and at others underweigh, about fifteen miles to the westward of Duck Island. Yesterday a fine breeze sprung up from the E.N.E. when a great alteration took place in the ice. Today plying to windward, fine clear weather, the grand fleet in company and in sight.

Thursday 30th. Since last date the weather has been alternately thick and clear with chiefly light breezes from the N.E. and E.N.E. Ship occasionally made fast as convenient. Little or no alteration in the ice to be perceived. Today the *Brunswick* and *Truelove* got out from among the floes; swell from the south.

Friday July 1st. Ship plying south, Wind about S.S.E.

Monday 4th. Ship dodging. Latter part made fast to a floe piece, wind N.E. and thick, *Neptune* of London and the *Polar Star*, French ship, in coy. On Saturday we got the northerly breeze when we ran till Sunday night with studding sails. Supposed distance from the land eighty miles. Lat. 71° 30'. Ice appeared slack before it came on thick. The thirteen sail that were among the ice to the northward had come out again. On Sunday spoke the *Wm. Lee*, one of that number. It is generally agreed that some heavy gales are wanting before a north west passage be got.

From Tuesday 5th to Friday 8th. Ship plying to the northward along the ice. On Friday night the wind came from the S.W. when we run until Sunday morning with studding sails when we came abreast Duck Islands.

Sunday 10th. Ship dodging about five miles to the westward of Duck Islands. Strong breeze from the S.W. with thick weather and showers twenty four sails in sight four miles to the north. The vessels that we had left north when we run south had proceeded north the preceeding Thursday.

Monday 11th. Fine breeze from the N.E. Ship plying to windward amongst loose floes and pieces of ice. At 8 p.m. saw a number of our fleet proceeding north and the appearance of much land water to the north. Set studding sails [ie. stunsails] and run north to suit the leads; the windy weather increasing very much from the S.W.

Tuesday 12th. At two o'clock this morning it increased to heavy gale from the S.W. By this time we were about twenty miles in amongst the ice. A large hole of water still remaining. Double-reefed our topsails and plyed to windward. Towards miday [sic] the ice closed rapidly, when we were obliged to fall down upon the lee ice. In doing so got along side the *Neptune* of Aberdeen and carried away three of his boats and damaged two of our own. During the afternoon had several severe pressures upon our vessel, indeed so much so that we expected to become a wreck. About two o'clock saw the *Neptune* of London become a wreck. In the course of six or eight hours the hull entirely disapeared (sic) under the ice. About midnight the gale gradually abated.

Wednesday 13th. Weather clear, fine breeze from the N.E. ship made fast to a floe. The ice opened at noon, got underweigh, and towed to the north. At 6 p.m. wind came from the south with showers of snow, took our boats up set studding sails and ran north. About midnight made fast to the land ice; eight or ten sail in compy.

Thursday 14th. At two this morning obliged to unmoor in order to avoid the *Ld. Gambier* driving upon us. The wind had now increased to a heavy gale from the S.W., a hole of water still remaining. Double reefed our topsails and plyed to windward. The press of sail we carried was very great and was what few of the ships could do; after plying to windward so long as we could we were obliged to run upon the lee ice at 2 p.m. which fortunately was broken up, and in detached pieces. Notwithstanding the other ships keeping their moorings longer than us, they were even compelled to take the lee ice even before us, sixteen sail visible to the north previous to the gale.

Friday 15th. The gale has now abated and light variable airs. Ship lying as before, have had no press upon us. *Ellison* of Hull close to us, floes seem very light and much broken up, but a great number of bergs around us. Heard that six of the men belonging to the *Neptune* of London had died from the effects of liquor (false). Suppose in lat. 75⁰ N, twelve miles from the land.

Saturday 16th. Light breezes from E.S.E. and clear ship still beset. Lat. by obs. 75⁰ 13'N.

Sunday 17th. Fine breeze from the N.E., weather alternately thick and clear. Ships in compy. as before observed, the sixteen sail to the north. Lat. 74⁰ 58'N. The *Ingria* and French ship have had a very great pressure, but still safe.

Monday 18th. Cloudy weather fresh breezes from the S.W. with showers of snow. Ship lying free from pressure; ice closing gradually.

Tuesday 19th. Fine clear weather with a fine breeze from the N.E. Ice opening in the morning got underweigh and ran south, but the floes being blocked by icebergs we only got a mile or two by night.

Wednesday 20th. In the morning made fast to a berg aground. Fresh breezes from the N.E. with thick fogs; the ice driving south at a rapid rate, but being so blocked with bergs we could get no opportunity of proceeding south. The nine sail still in company; at night cast off from the berg and dodged in a hole of water.

Thursday 21st. Hazey [sic] weather, wind at midnight veered around to S.W., now blows a moderate breeze. Ship dodging under the lee of a large floe to which the other ships are made fast. The three ships that were in the ice to the southward of us we have lost sight of, and leaves little doubt but that they have got into the south water. They are the *Kiero*, *Cove* and *Bon-accord*. The fifteen sail are quite visible to the northward. A passage in that direction is now abandoned and our endeavours are directed to the south first opportunity.

Friday 22nd. Hazey [sic] with a fresh breeze from the S.W. Ship made fast to a floe; same vessels still in company.

Saturday 23rd. This morning the wind veered round to the N.E., light airs and fine weather. Cast off and made for the south, the ice being broke up and in the manner of pack ice we warped, towed etc. with all our people. At night we had got only about two miles south from where we cast off.

Sunday 24th. Fine clear weather with light airs from the northward. Ship made fast the greater part of this day. In the afternoon the ice opened, called all hands and tracked and warped ship south. The south water in sight. Lat. by obs. 74⁰ 45'.

Monday 25th. Weather thick and hazey (sic). Moderate breezes from the S.W. After endeavouring until this afternoon we gained the south water just in time to save ourselves from being blocked in the ice with the southerly breeze. We left beset near the edge of the ice the *Ingria*, *Margaret* and *Neptune* and the Frenchmen; the *Ellison* etc, had got out some hours previous. I went this evening in one of the boats in pursuit of a bear. I fired, there being a short swell on, hit him only in the shoulder, this served but to enrage the savage animal. We pulled close upon it and after a great many attempts at last succeeded in killing it. During this time the bear had three different time his paws and teeth on the boats gunwale, but we managed to repel him with different weapons, the lances being bad was the chief cause of our taking so long to kill it.

Tuesday 26th. Fine clear weather. Fresh breeze from the S.W. Ship plying south among straggling ice, and numbers of bergs. Land distant about twenty miles. Lat. 74⁰ 20'.

Wednesday 27th. Fine weather with fine northerly breezes; ship running south with all sail set, sails in sight and coy.

Thursday 28th. Fine breezes from the E.N.E. with fine weather. Ship running south lat. 73⁰ N.

Friday 29th. Cloudy weather with a fresh breeze from the N.E. Ship running along the ice; at night hauled in to a deep bight. Saw a ship which bore down to us. Turned out to be the *Lee* of Hull with eight fish, 135 tons of oil. He, Mr Lee, informed us that our distance form the west land was about eighty five miles. He had been there but could not proceed north on account of the ice; few fish were seen. He could plainly distinguish the North water, and endeavouring to gain it he accidentally got drove out into the east water where we at first saw him. The southerly gales that we experienced in Melville Bay were not felt at the west side where he was. The wind from that quarter would now be the most likely circumstance to stream the ice off from the west land and make us a passage. Lat. at noon 71⁰ 55'N.

Saturday 30th. Cloudy weather with snow showers; fresh breeze at N.E. Ship plying along the outskirts of the ice, seven ships in coy. Lat. 71⁰ 30'.

Sunday 31st. Dull cloudy weather with frequent showers of small snow. Fresh breezes from the N.E. – Ship dodging at the edge of the ice, several ships in compy. Spoke the *Ingria* at 3 p.m.; run south along the ice.

Monday 1st August. Cloudy weather with light winds at E.N.E. Early this morning hauled our wind. Now plying along the ice. Observed in lat. 70⁰ 48'N.

Tuesday 2nd. Thick foggy weather light winds at E.N.E. and N.E. Ship plying and dodging at the edge of the ice.

Wednesday 3rd. Fine clear weather with a moderate breeze from the W.N.W. Ship plying to windward along the ice; several strange sail to leeward. Can distinguish the *Commet* [sic ie. *Comet*], one of the vessels that was among the middle fleet in Melville Bay, which circumstance makes us suppose that this fleet has made their way out of the bay into the south water, no prospect being to the northward. Lat. at noon 70° 48'N.

Thursday 4th. Light variable airs and fine weather. At 8 p.m. the breeze freshned [sic] from S.W. when we plyed south along the ice. *Truelove, Commet, Harmony* etc. in. company. Lat. 70° 12'N.

Friday 5th. Fine clear weather. Fresh breezes from the W.N.W. Ship plying along the ice; about twenty sail in sight and company. Lat. by obs. 70° 8'N.

Saturday 6th. Fine clear weather; light winds from the W.S.W. Early this morning rounded the south end of the ice, to all appearance. Ship reaching N.W. by N. lat. At 3 p.m. fell in with ice, tacked; wind N.E. A fresh breeze in the evening, thick weather, ship reaching to the N.N.W.

Sunday 7th. Thick weather with occasional blinks. Ship among rank ice boring from W.N.W. to N.N.W., wind variable and light.

Monday 8th. Thick weather. Ship dodging and plying among floes and pieces of ice. Wind northerly, light breezes, *Earl Percy* in coy. Lat. by obs. 68° 46'.

Tuesday 9th. Fore part thick foggy weather, in the afternoon cleared up. Saw the land supposed distance forty miles. Wind northerly varies from E.N.E. to N., a strong breeze. Ship plying and reaching the N.W. in the evening. Could get no further for ice forty miles distant. Some very large fields of ice, but no whales seen.

Wednesday 10th. Fine clear weather with a moderate breeze from the north. Ship reaching to the E.S.E., so as to get clear of the ice and proceed north. *Earl Percy* in compny.

Thursday 11th. Light airs and calm. Fine warm weather. Lat. 69°8'N.

Friday 12th. Clear weather, fore part a fine breeze from the S.S.E. Ship reaching to E. and E.N.E., after part light variable airs and calms. Ship at the edge of the ice.

Saturday 13th. Fine clear weather and a fine breeze at S.S.W. Ship reaching E. and E.N.E along the ice, *Earl Percy* and *Madamoiselle* in compy. Lat. by obs. 69° 56' N.

Sunday 14th. Cloudy weather. Wind S.S.W., ship reaching along the ice *Earl Percy* etc. in co.

Monday 15th and Tuesday 16th. Southerly breezes. Ship running along the ice latter day. Lat. 72°.

Wednesday. A brisk gale from the S.W., fore part ship plying to windward at the ice edge. Midday cleared a little, and an opening in the ice offering wore ship and run N.N.W., and in a few hours thick fog again. Fell in with the ice, very rank chiefly bay ice. *Earl Percy* in coy.

Thursday 18th. Thick foggy weather. Moderate breezes from the S.W. Ship among the ice.

Friday 19th. Fore part thick weather, wind southerly. Miday [sic] cleared, wind to E.N.E. Ship reaching to the S.E. and from among the ice. Again met our two partners, viz. the *Earl Percy* and Frenchman. At 6 p.m. got clear of the ice and ran to the south along the ice. Lat. at noon 72° 20'.

Saturday 20th. Dark cloudy weather. At 8 a.m. took the ice, it appearing to be slack. Wind S.E. at noon, met with a stoppage, tacked and plyed to the eastward. Wind S.S.W. thick fogg [sic]. At 8 p.m. got clear of the ice.

Sunday 21st. Thick foggy weather with occasional blinks. Wind variable but northerly. Ship plying to windward, ice in sight, one ship also. Lat. 71^0 40'.

Monday 22nd. Fore part moderate breezes from the N.N.W., afternoon west. Weather alternately thick and clear, ship plying. Ice seems to have been much parted from the recent southerly winds; a bark in sight. Lat. 71^0 20'.

Tuesday 23rd. Weather thick with occasional blinks. Fine fresh breezes from the S.W. At 8 a.m. having got into deep bight in the ice, and the ice appearing much parted, we run to the N.N.W. and N.W. to suit the leads; so ends. Ship running as before among heavy straggling sconce pieces and floes. *Earl Percy* and Frenchman in sight at 9 a.m.

Wednesday 24th. Weather as before. Wind S.E. ship dodging when thick and running to the N.N.W. and N.W. when clear; heavy floes and straggling pieces with much water.

Thursday 25th. Weather alternately thick and clear, a fresh breeze from the E.N.E. This forenoon reached to the N.W. and came to the land ice. Saw seven sail made fast, and some dodging at the edge. Spoke the *Alfred*; they were part of the fleet that got separated from us in the East water. They rounded the north end of the ice in lat. 73^0 N; few or no fish had been seen by them. We had also some intelligence of the north ships from Mr. Brass. At noon saw the land distance about thirty miles, ship plying to the north among floes and straggling ice in lat. 70^0 20'. The seven ships run south together with a few more from the north that passed us in the evening.

Friday 26th. Weather as before. Wind varies from E.N.E. to N.N.E. Ship plying to the northward, land distant about thirty miles. At 3 a.m. spoke the *Eliza Swan*. They informed us the North fleet had rounded the ice north on the 16th July, and of the success of their fishery which was only poor. No loss of ships however had happened (See list for success of ships). Lat. 70^0 38'.

Saturday 27th. Cloudy weather. Moderate breeze from the E.N.E. Ship plying to windward, afternoon reaching to the east, at noon land distant thirty miles, with large floes intervening. Lat. 70^0 54'.

Sunday 28th. Clear weather with a fine breeze from the S.W. Ship running N.E. by E. At 8 p.m. breeze failed us, land distant about sixty miles (shaping, hoping [?] find floes and ice in afternoon – this section an addition).

Monday 29th. A smart gale form the N.N.E. with cloudy weather. Ship reaching to the east, a heavy swell. Lat. 72^0 43'N.

Tuesday 30th. A moderate breeze from the eastward with thick foggs [sic]. Ship reaching N.N.E.

Wednesday 31st. Gale as before, ship reaching north.

Thursday September 1st. Clear weather and strong breeze at E.N.E. this morning; at eight a.m. tacked about ten miles from the land. Lat. 72^0.

Friday 2nd and Saturday 3rd. Light variable airs and calms with snow showers.

Sunday 4th. Thick hazey (sic) weather and showers, with a strong breeze from S.W. to south. Ship running north with a press of sail.

Monday 5th. Winds and weather, ditto. At 9 a.m. tacked at an extent of pack, ice bergs very numerous. Lat. supposed in 75° 30'N. Saw an island bearing N.E., distance about twelve miles.

Tuesday 6th. Wind etc. as before. At 9 a.m. run along the ice, saw land bearing from N.E. to S.E. appearing, as islands distance about twelve miles. At 2 p.m. hauled to the wind, no fish seen. At 3 p.m. again to the N.N.W.; at 6 p.m. saw a headland. Supposed to be Cape York.

Wednesday 7th. Weather cold and cloudy with frequent showers; ship reaching N.W.

Thursday 8th. Clear frosty weather. Wind varied in course of the day from W.S.W. to S.S.E. Ship reaching as winds permit. Lat. at noon 74° N.

Friday 9th. Fine clear weather, ship running S.W. with studding sails. Lat. 73° 11' North.

Saturday 10th. Cloudy with showers. Ship running south. Lat. at noon 72° N.

Sunday 11th. Cloudy weather. Moderate winds from the north, ship running south but more towards the land.

Monday 12th. Fine clear weather ship running W.N.W. with light winds from the N.N.E.; no land seen yet. Lat. 70° 4'N.

Tuesday 13th. Moderate breezes from the northw'd and cloudy. Ship running towards the land past several heavy streams of ice. Lat. 69° 20'.

Wednesday 14th. A gale at N.E. with cloudy weather and snow showers. This morning made Cape Bisson. Today ship running along the land to the south. In the evening hauled our wind abreast of Home bay land distant twelve miles.

Thursday 15th. Strong winds from the northw'd and cloudy. Ship plying to windward among heavy pieces of ice and bergs; *Alfred* in coy. Lat. 68° 40.

Friday 16th. A moderate breeze from the northward, still cloudy. Saw the land distant ten miles, ship running south. Evening becalmed, twenty sail in sight.

Saturday 17th to Tuesday 20th. Has been clear frosty weather with moderate winds from the northward. Ship plying and dodging among streams of ice near the land in lat. 68° 30' and a number of ships in coy. and sight. Our boats have been in with the land three times, but have had no success. Have seen several fish and some also captured by different ships. Heard of the loss of the *Rambler* of Kircaldy (sic) in about lat. 68° 45'N, close to the land being jamed [sic] between the floes.

Wednesday 21st. Fine clear weather with light variable airs; this morning all boats away after fish. At 11 a.m. one of them got fast W.W. at ¹/₂ past 12, dead about five along side and begun to flench. [Here a whale captured sign]. Distance from the land ten miles; a number of ships in coy. Lat. about 68° 10'N.

Wednesday 28th. Since the 21st has been clear frosty weather with moderate and variable breezes. Ship dodging and plying in the vicinity of Brodie Bay. Today becalmed abreast of Cape Searl [e]; have seen no fish since the 22nd. Several ships have bore up for home. Here there is a heavy pack between us and the land of six or eight miles in breadth, which extends as far at the north as Cape Broughton.

Saturday 1st October. Since 28th has been generally moderate and clear, and strong frosty weather. Winds prevail from the north with a heavy swell upon the land. Ship plying and dodging about ten miles to the southw'd of Cape Searle. Several vessels in compy. seemingly making arrangements for home, the ice lies close to the land and is in the state of brasshy [sic] pack, so that together with the bay ice that forms amongst it, renders the possibility of securing a fish, even although struck, extremely problematical. Tonight about 6 p.m. had the misfortune to have one of our Orkneymen pitched overboard from off the bowsprit, every exertion being made proved in vain from the heavy swell etc.

Sunday 2nd. Heavy gales from the N.E. and cloudy at noon; wore ship and run to the S.W. So ends.

Then follow seven sides which are blank, have faint drawings or partly legible notes: 1, blank except headed by note in pencil – "continued, mention that by their united endeavours they captured whales"; 2, sketch of spear (?); 3, blank; 4, shadowy sketch of terrain; 5, 6 pages largely removed; 7, draft of a report (written in pencil) assessing prospects for early arrival on the whaling grounds:-

Mention that the number of whales captured at the east side fishing amounted to ( ). The early and flattering prospects of last year biased the commanders, I believe, in favour of proceeding early to the north, but their prospects were blighted on reaching the lat. of 74^0. On the 17th June, when the grand fleet were moored in the neighbourhood of Baffins 3 Island waiting an opportunity of proceeding north, I went on shore and proceeded to the greater elevation of the island in company with a number of the commanders when, with the aid of glasses and matured judgements, the state of the country was considered as very discouraging, presenting as far as the eye could reach nothing but a solid sheet of ice interspersed with numberless icebergs. Time now rolled on in merely providing for the safeguard of the vessels, and in cruising about in search of an opening and much [?] most [?] vessels was experimenting [?] investigating [?] – for an alteration in the ice. By the beginning of July the patience of the majority of the commanders was worn out in their endeavour for a passage to the north, accordingly at this time sail made all expedition to the south to ascertain if their [sic] was any change/chance [?] prospect in that direction, leaving commanders of the fleet still looking for a northerly opening. However when this southward bound fleet reached the lat. where a passage is usually looked for, it was found that the prospect was as much, if not more, discouraging there than where they had just left. Consequently [as] any vessel hastened again to ascertain if any alteration had taken place in the state of the north ice when they [two illegible words here] found that an alteration had taken place, and that those who stopt [sic] behind had taken advantage of it, and were now out of sight, and beyond the possibility of the others joining them from a sudden closing of the ice. On the 12th, the south fleet had now divided into two, and were advanced to some distance among the ice when they were taken with a tremendous gale from the S.W. Numbers of the ships suffered prodigious pressure, but all with one exception escaped, viz. *Neptune* of London. The wreck of the ill–fated vessel I had the misfortune to witness being only about three quarters of a mile from it, but it would be needless to trouble you with a particular detail from the resemblance [?] to last year's account. Suffice is it to say that after the first melancholy sight it, in a few hours, entirely disappeared under the ice. Two lives were lost during the transaction from intemperance and exposure. The vessels that accomplished the north passage were not particularly successful, a few only making any considerable captures. The south fleet found it impossible to get a north passage, so made all exertion and proceeded to the south. This latter passage was accomplished about the end of August. You will be able to see from your returns and by comparing it with the number stated to have been got at the [sketch – see pl.18] east side the success of the coastland fishing. Our vessel left the country on the third of October I was informed in Edinburgh that the number of whales got in October would about equal the number got during the former part [?] of the season (this however I could settle, satisfactorily by a further investigation of the matter). The number of wrecks that occurred this season were three viz. the *James* of Peterhead, *Neptune* of London and *Rambler* of Kircaldy (sic), the former early in the season about the lat. of 72^0 North among the floes and without anything remarkable attending the disaster. The *Rambler* was lost about lat. 68^0; I was informed that it was very sudden, so much so that the surgeon and mate were obliged to swim for their lives. The weather was chiefly characterized by the great proportion of thick fogs, few gales of wind occurred, light and moderate northerly breezes predominating. I may here mention that the wreck of the *Harmony* of Hull, who sailed for the straits two months previous to any other vessel, would discourage any such inconsistent experiments again.

The account I received from the surgeon of the *John* of Greenock of their adventure and suffering of the boat's crew, of which he made one of the number that left the vessel for the pur[sic] I will briefly state he mentioned that they left the vessel with the agreement of those left on board, and proceeded on their half desperate and enterprizing excursion, but when only about two miles distant, for they made but slow progress, [author's footnote here – or so near the peculiar dress of an individual upon the rigging could me made out], they observed that the vessel began to move from them, when immediately they made signals that they intended again to return and join their ship.

A faint sketch with a list of ships
    Abram
    Ariel – 0
    Alfred
    Andrew Marvel (sic)
    Brunswick – 2
On opposite page sketch of bridge with figures [pl. 25].

18. *Vessel trapped in the ice . Compare with Gibson drawing (pl. 13), number four which identifies it as the* **Three Brothers** *of Dundee.*

*19. Vessel in the ice, crew camping along side. Compare with Gibson drawing (pl. 13), number 3, which identifies it as the **Alexander** of Aberdeen.*

*20. Compare with Gibson drawing (pl. 13) number 5, which identifies it as the **William**, confirmed by the next drawing in the sequence (pl. 21).*

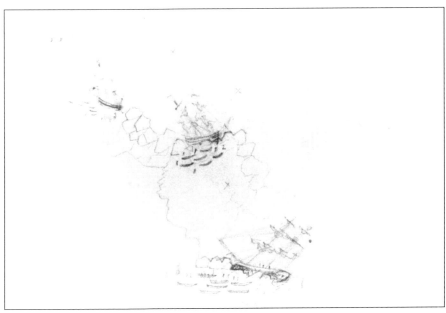

21. Small scale sketch which show the **Gilder, North Briton, Alexander, Three Brothers** *and* **William** *(name inscribed below).*

22. Sketch of whaling ship down at the stern, and of an iceberg.

63

*23. Port profile view of whaling vessel. Compare with drawing of **Zephyr** in the Gibson drawing.*

24. Unidentified Scottish scene showing a man and a woman crossing a stone bridge.

25. *Thumb nail sketch of whaleships trapped in the ice.*

8. LOGIE O'BUCHAN

O! Logie o'Buchan,- O! Logie the laird,
They hae taken away Jamie that delved in the yard,
Who played on the pipe wi' the viol sae sma',
Thae hae ta'en away Jamie the flower of them a':
He said, think na long lassie, tho I gang awa'
For the summer is coming, cauld winter awa'
I'll come back and see thee, in spite of them a'.

Sandy has arisen, has gaer, and has kye,
A house, and a haddin [?], and siller for bye,
But I'd tak mine ain lad wi' his staff in his hand
Before I'd hae him wi' his houses and land
                              He said etc.
My daddy looks sulky, my mither looks sour,
They frown upon Jamie, because he is poor,
Tho' I loo him as weel as a daughter should do
They're nae sae dear to me, Jamie, as you.
                              He said etc.

I sit on my creepie, and spin at my wheel,
And think on the laddy that loo'd me sae weel,
He had but a sixpence, he breake it in twa,
And he goed me the half o't when he went awa.

Then haste ye back, Jamie, and bide na awa,
Then haste ye back, Jamie, and bide na awa
Summer is coming, cauld winters awa
And ye'll come and see me, in spite o the a'.

9. DESCRIPTION OF MEDICAL TREATMENT GIVEN TO BOURMASTER SPENCE

About the 20th April, Bourmaster Spence applied to me, having received a fall upon on his right shoulder in consequence of the ship giving a heavy lurch, which hurried him from the weather side against the bulwark. He had received the injury eight or ten days previous to any complaint to me, during which time he had attended ship's duty. He complained of pain in his shoulder with regard to motion. Suffice it to say that ever since he had received the injury he had undergone the ordinary labour of sailor in stormy weather, and at the time I was aquainted could move his arm in various directions, even lifting his hand to the back of his head. There was no obvious distortion, and the pain was seated chiefly in and round the shoulder joint; a slight degree of swelling was also present. From the symptoms etc. I therefore concluded it to be a severe contusion. I did not employ local bleeding, the severity of the inflamation [sic], if it had so prevailed at first, having subsided. Indeed I was destitute of the means of doing so, having neither leeches nor cupping aparatus [sic] on board.

He could not bear the thought of being confined below, general bleeding was therefore not employed, indeed the symptoms did not imperiously call its exhibition. Friction with anodyne linniment [sic] was therefore employed as his attention to duty rendered the employment of any other means abortive. He continued going on much in the same way, using the friction with anodyne and stimulating liniments. We made the south west ice on the 6th May, and had been employed in the fishery he never was absent from his duty, such as rowing in the boats, forking blubber, etc. On the 8th June I applied a blister over the shoulder joint and confined him below, he having complained of augmented pain. No abatement of the symptoms followed its application. On the 14th he began to complain of some difficulty in breathing with an occasional tickling cough, accompanied with pain under the axilla over the 4th, 5th and 6th ribs. I therefore blead [sic] him to the extent of fifteen ounces, and over the seat of the pain I put a large strengthening plaster. A bandage round the chest and across the shoulders had been applied some days previous on account of the complaint in the shoulder. This treatment produced some abatement of this complaint. At night he got thirty drops of Tinct. Opii., which procured him some hours of sleep.

June 15th. This morning took the dose of salts which had operated, but found very little abatement of the difficulty of breathing pain, and at noon took fifteen ounces of blood which procured a further diminution of the pain and difficult respiration. The pulse was now soft and beat sixty in a minute. At night the pain became excessive so as to produce fainting, with spasm and starting in the muscles which occasionally intermitted. At 10 p.m. gave 2 grs. Opium and 3 grs. of camphor. Combined pulse all along pretty regular.

June 16th. This morning saw him. He had experienced a tolerable night, the opiate having procured a little sleep and the pain in the shoulder somewhat abated. At 8 a.m. applied a blister over the seat of the pain, and gave him 4 grs. calomel and 2 grs. opium combined. In the afternoon ordered Sulph. Magnesia, 6 drachms Tart. Antimon. Grss [?] in Aqua.Menth., 8 ounces Liqr., two tablespoonfuls every hour. This solution produced a copious stool in the evening. At bedtime gave him Tinct. Opii [ix drops?]. Pulse natural, his breathing and pain rather easier.

June 17th. This morning found him much in the same state. The opiate had procured him a little rest. At 8 a.m. he had another attack of the convulsive spasms which soon abated and left him much in the same state as before. At noon gave him Calomel Grs. iv – Pulv. Rhei. Grs.v – Pulv. Zingil Grs. iii. minims; in the afternoon he had another attack of the convulsive spasms, pulse sixty & natural. In the evening repeated the blister on the fore part of the shoulder. Pain in the joint still severe at bedtime; gave him Tinct. Opii. Grs ix [drops].

June 18th. Saw him this morning; pain still continued and severe – pulse sixty and natural. He passed a tolerable night. Appetite a little improved – repeated the solution of Sulph. Magnesia ut antea [as before], pain rather easier, pulse regular. At bed time opiate as before with 3 grs. calomel combined.

June 19th. Found him this morning rather easier, pulse natural. Had passed a pretty good night; appetite rather improved. In the forenoon gave him Calomel Grs. iv Pulv. Rhei. Grs v Zingil. Grs iii minims. Shortly after had a stool in the evening, had an exacerbation of pain in the shoulder. Applied another blister at bed time, repeated the opiate with 3 grs. Calomel. Combined pulse rather fuller.

June 20th. Saw him this morning. Had passed a tolerable night, pain rather easier, pulse softer. Ordered the saline solution to be administered when awake, but having complained of nausea precluded its exhibition. Since yesterday afternoon has had three natural stools. Repeated the opiate with Calomel Grs. iii, Pulv. Antimonalis Grs. v combined at bedtime.

June 21st. Pain rather easier, pulse natural. Had another stool, was removed out of bed in the afternoon for a quarter of an hour, repeated the opiate with 3 grs. Calomel, Pulv. Antimon. Grs. V minim at bedtime.

June 22nd. Has passed a tolerable night, pulse natural. Bowels regular and appears upon the whole much better today. At night repeated the opiate.

June 23rd. Had passed a tolerable night and continued much in the same state at night; repeated the opiate.

June 24th. Complains still of severe pain. Gave him a laxative powder and put on a blister on the back part of the joint. At night blead (sic) him to the extent of twelve ounces. Having had another severe attack of the spasmodic convulsions, which produced a slight cessation of the pain and brought the pulse to a natural standard, which before had been rather strong and full at night. Repeated the opiate with 3 grs. Calomel and 5 grs. Pulv. Antimonialis combined.

June 25th. Complains still of severe pain. Had passed a sleeples [sic] night. Gave 4 grs. Calomel 5 grs. Pulv. Rhei. and 2 grs. Pulv. Zingil. combined. This afternoon was visited by Mr. Aitkin, surgeon of the *William* of Hull who concurred with me in opinion that it was a case of inflammation of the joint. In the forenoon gave $2\frac{1}{2}$ grs. Opium, 3 Calomel combined, but without the least relief.

June 26th, 27th. Still complained of severe pain and strangury caused by the blister, for which I gave him plentiful drinks, barley water with opiate.

28th. Today, the Calomel given in combination with the opiates, although cautiously administered, produced, a swelling of the gums with a flow of saliva for which I gave a purge with an astringent gargle.

In cases of extreme debility in females

Ry Ammon Carb –   drachms
   Aqua Menth Virid –   fluid ounces
   Tinct.Cardam.Comp - ounces

Two or three tablespoonfuls of the mixture may be taken two or three times a day.

10. NAMES

R ough sketch of ships in ice [pl. 26] and a list of names:-

Wm. Jack [or Tait]
Wm. Johnstone
Hugh Yanson
James Holland
Wm. Sclater
Magnus Carson
James Fawlis
Wm. Stanger
John Millar
Thom. Stanger
Alexr. McKinnon
Wm. Smith
Wm. Linskill
John Hunter

Peter Slocund
James Forth
Robert Harvey
Alexr. More
Wm. Sclater
Malcolm Sinclair
David Honiston
John Tait
Hugh Rendall 2

Blank page opposite the letter; then overleaf:-

[Signatures of] James Sherwood Harpooner – George Laing on board of the Ship *Volunteer* Davis Straits.

11. PENCIL NOTES

Also sketch of a bird with faint inscription: Seen in 63 North lat. Size of a common crow. [See pl. 2a]

On the final page is a note in pencil. (barely legible) expanding the journal entries for 11th –15th June, 1831:-

Saturday 11th. Weather thick winds E.N.E., ship made fast to an iceberg about a gunshot from the southern of Buchan Isles.
Sunday 12th. Fine clear weather light southerly airs. About midnight got underweigh and tacked sth [?] to the southward.
Monday 13th. Ship made fast to a floe, will [?] get no further, a final [?] stoppage only intervening between us and the southward water. On Tuesday 15th at night got through the bar and ship made fast at our present situation about 8 p.m. after. Today had visit from the surgeon of *John* of Greenock who related to us the vicissitudes they had experienced [?].

12. SHIPS OF THE ARCTIC FLEET 1830-1831

The ships listed here are those mentioned in Laing's journals.

Abram of Hull.   From 1824-1832 Capt. William Jackson, brother-in-law of William Scoresby jnr. Bark built at Lancaster 1806.   Purchased by William Mercer and John Tidd of Gainsborough in the firm of Tidd, Mercer and Co. Prevented by southerly winters and thick weather from entering Davis Strait in 1831. Wintered over in Arctic in disastrous 1835 season. Joined Kirkcaldy fleet after 1853 and still operating from there in 1862.

Achilles of Dundee.   Captain Thomas replaced Captain Valentine 1830.   One of two Dundee ships lost of fleet of nine ships.

Alexander of Aberdeen.   The second vessel fitted out by the Admiralty in 1818 under the command of Captain John Ross, explored Baffin Bay and further west in search of the North West Passage.   In the Aberdeen fleet from 1819.   Under the command of Captain Allan in 1830.   Lost within sight of *Zephyr* in 1830. One of four ships lost of fleet of ten Aberdeen ships.

Alfred of Hull.   303 tons.   Built in Whitehaven, Cumbria, 1796.   Registered at Hull 1811.   Belonged to Gardiner and Joseph Egginton by 1825.   William Brass, an extremely experienced whaleman, her commander 1830-1835.   Brought home eighty tons of oil from five whales in 1830, and eighty five tons from five whales in 1831.   Transferred to Bo'ness in 1836.   Lost 1847.

Andrew Marvell of Hull.   377 tons.   Built in Hull, 1812 for Captain John Marshall, ship owner.   Owned by Thomas Jackson, Thomas Harrison Marshall and Richard Marshall, 1825-1833.   Commanded by Captain Orton, 1830, returned clean.   Under Captain Wright in 1831 brought home fifty five tons of oil from four whales.

Ariel of Hull.   Active in the Hull fleet 1799-1807 and 1817-32.   Home clean in 1830 under command of Captain Rogers.   Captain Linskill's catch in 1831, ten tons of oil from one whale.

Baffin of Leith.   Launched 1820 and first registered at Liverpool.   The only truly purpose-built British whaler and the first whaling ship built by Mottershead and Hays, Liverpool as command for Captain William Scoresby Jnr. who charted the coast of Greenland in 1822.   His account of this voyage, *Journal of a Voyage to the Northern Whale Fishery*, published in 1823.   Under command of Captain Smith from 1823, and sailed with Leith fleet from 1827.   Lost 1830.

Bon-Accord of Aberdeen. 363 tons. Built for the Bon Accord Whale Fishing Company, 1813. Under command of Captain Parker until 1839. Brought home seventeen tons of oil from one whale in 1830 and ninety tons from six whales in 1831. Sold to Hull, 1843-44.

Brunswick of Hull built at Paull on the Humber in 1814 for James Shrapnell Bowden and Benjamin Wright. By 1824 her owners were James and William Bowden, and William Blyth her master from 1814-1816 and 1818-1834. Her catch in 1830 was eighty nine tons from six whales and one hundred tons from seven whales in 1831. Lost in 1842 while trading.

Caledonia of Kirkcaldy. In 1830 the fleet comprised five ships and Captain Todd brought home one hundred and six tons of oil from eight whales. In 1831 the catch was thirty tons from two whales – six ships in the fleet.

Comet of Hull. 303 tons. Built at Rotherhithe 1791. In the whaling trade 1823-1840. By 1826 in the hands of Thomas Jackson, Thomas Harrison Marshall and Richard Marshall and others. Sole owner from 1829 Thomas Barkworth, until lost while trading in 1843. Under the command of Captain Charles Woodhall in 1830, thirteen tons of oil from one whale. Captain John Markham master of the *Volunteer* in 1829-30 was in command of the *Comet*, in 1831 produced thirty five tons of oil from three whales.

Cove of Newcastle. Built at Whitby in 1798. 374 tons. Captain George Palmer who founded Palmer shipyard on the Tyne at Jarrow, in command from 1815-1833. In 1830 when the fleet comprised of three vessels, catch yielded eighty tons of oil from five whales captured. Took thirty tons from two whales in 1831 when fleet of four ships. On 24th July 1831 took on board seven men from the lost *Neptune* of London. Sold to Hull in 1834 where owned by Samuel Cooper and William Spyvee Cooper. In 1836 *Cove* selected to search for whalers forced to over winter in the Arctic. Lost in trade in 1836.

Cumbrian of Hull. Built at South Shields in 1811. To Hull fleet from Newcastle in 1819; owned by James Shrapnell Bowden, George Silvester Wright, merchants and William Blyth, master mariner. Came home clean under command of Captain Martin Munro in 1830 and in 1831 twelve tons of oil from one whale. Lost 1844 while trading.

Dorothy of Dundee. In fleet of nine ships in 1830, Captain Davidson brought home thirty two tons of oil from two whales and in 1831 ninety tons of oil from eight whales.

Duncombe of Hull. 270 tons. Built at Thorne 1800 and in Hull fleet from 1801 and briefly captured by French privateer in 1804. Owners Spyvee and Cooper. Captain Scoffin master in 1826 and assisted in saving *Eagle* in 1830, returning home clean. Forced to over winter in Arctic in 1835, last voyage in fishery 1837. To Stockton in 1845.

Eagle of Hull. Built at Sutton 1813. Owners 1825-1835 Robert Gibson and William Gibson, William Thomas, merchant. Captain Wright, her master, in 1830 brought home catch of seven whales yielding fifty four tons of oil. Master in 1831 Captain Chester who was prevented by conditions from entering Davis Straits so fished Greenland waters, with catch of seven whales yielding forty eight tons of oil. Last voyage in Hull whaling fleet in 1833. Sold to Kings Lynn in 1848.

Earl Percy of Kirkcaldy. Sole whaler of Kirkcaldy in 1813, Captain Cunningham, Captain Stewart in command 1830-1833. Home clean in 1830 when fleet comprised of five ships and with eleven tons of oil from one whale in fleet of six ships in 1831. Last year in fishery 1837.

Eclipse of Peterhead. Generally known as the "Old Eclipse". Joined fleet in 1820. Under command of well known Peterhead masters Souttar 1820-26, 1832-1836, William Penny 1826-32, and later J. Gray who discovered and named Eclipse Sound in 1854. Fleet of thirteen ships in 1830, catch of two whales making eighteen tons of oil. Clean in 1831 when fleet of twelve ships. Lost 1858.

Egginton of Kirkcaldy. 336 tons. Built in Paull, near Hull, for the twin brothers Gardiner and Joseph Egginton, the moguls of the Hull whaling trade in its heyday. First voyage to the Arctic in 1787 and was one of the best fished vessels in Arctic fleet in many seasons. Sold to London owners in 1824 but is not recorded as whaling from there. One of five vessels in Kirkcaldy fleet in 1830 and brought home thirteen and a half tons from one whale and the following year under the command of Captain Stoddart brought home fifty tons of oil from four whales. Lost in 1832 under Captain Todd.

Ellison of Hull. 349 tons. Built at Fishlake, Yorkshire, 1777 for Gardiner and Joseph Egginton, joined by James Allen and James Kiero Watson, banker, by 1825. In whaling trade from 1787-8 and 1796-1839. Under command of Captain Samuel Jackson whose catch in 1830 was six whales yielding eighty one tons of oil, in 1831 one whale yielded twelve tons of oil. Remained under ownership of Eggintons until lost while trading in 1846.

Eliza of Montrose a total wreck in 1803, but *Eliza Swan* operating out of the port as early as 1789. Captured by American frigate *President* (Commodore Rogers) in 1813 and ransomed for £5000. Many well fished seasons. One of four ships out of Montrose in 1830 came home clean under the command of Captain Fulton. He brought home eighty tons of oil from seven whales in 1831 – three ships in fleet. See Laing's list for success of ships.

Fairy of Dundee. Under command of Captain Welch in 1830 in fleet of nine ships brought home thirty one tons of oil from three whales and fifty tons of oil from four whales in 1831.

Gilder of Hull. Bark. 360 tons. Built at Paull in 1811 for William Shackles, linen draper, John Raines, merchant, and Joseph Sadler her first master. From 1821-22 her owners were Benjamin Stocks and Thomas Shackles, (who also shared ownership in the *Zephyr* with her master), and George Bunce, mariner and master. Captain James McKenzie took over command in 1827 and *Gilder* continued to be one of best fished whalers in Arctic fleet. Lost in sight of *Zephyr* in 1830.

Grenville Bay of Newcastle. Captain Wareham in command from joining the fleet in 1823. Of three ships out of Shields in 1830 he brought home sixty nine tons of oil from four whales. He took command of the *Lord Gambier* in 1831 and Captain Taylor brought home sixty tons of oil from five whales. Over-wintered in Arctic in 1835.

Harmony (I) of Hull. 293 tons. Built at Philadelphia for East India trade about 1786. A prize vessel in 1799 and registered at Hull in 1804. Registered to Thomas Bell, sole owner 1825. Under command of Captain Parker came home clean in 1830; incorrectly reported lost but in fact brought home thirty tons of oil from four whales in 1831. Sold to London in 1853.

Harmony (III) of Hull. Built at Whitby 1809. 378 tons. In Whitby fleet in 1827 and registered to Egginton brothers and James Allen of Hull in 1829. Under command of Captain Bramham brought home thirty eight tons of oil from two whales in 1830 and twenty tons from two whales the following year. Owners in 1833 Dikes and Gibson.

Hercules of Aberdeen also named *Aberdeen Greenlandman*, 248 tons. Built at Whitby in 1764. Joined Aberdeen fleet from London in 1784. Owned by Aberdeen Whale Fishing Company in 1798 and sole vessel in Aberdeen fleet. Captain Reid took command in 1827. Beset close to *Zephyr* in Melville Bay in 1830 and as one of ten ships in fleet brought home eleven tons of oil from one whale. Only five vessels in the fleet in 1834 when Aberdeen companies were advertising their ships and boiling yards for sale. *Hercules* diverted to the Atlantic timber trade in 1836.

Hope of Peterhead. 240 tons. The second vessel of Peterhead's whaling fleet commanded in 1802 by Captain Alexander Geary, member of one of the dominant Peterhead whaling families whose wife was a member of the Gray family, longer connected with Arctic whaling than any other family in the British Isles. One of two Peterhead ships lost in 1830 while under the command of Captain James Volum, master from 1825.

Horn of Dundee. In Dundee fleet in 1812. Captain Stevenson brought home twelve tons of oil from one whale in 1830, and seventy tons from six whales in 1831.

Ingria of Hull built at Whitby in 1803. Registered at Hull in 1809 to Samuel Cooper, shipowner and Alexander Webster, mariner. In 1823 principal owners were S. Cooper, William Spyvee Cooper and Thomas Hawkins. Under command of Captain Wilson in 1830 her crew came to the aid of the *Eagle* when that vessel stove. He brought home one hundred and six tons of oil from six whales and in 1831 the catch was three whales yielding thirty tons of oil. Lost at fishery 1833.

Isabella of Hull. Built at Hull in 1813 and registered to William Moxon, John White and Mallory Haslewood, mariner. In 1818 fitted out by the Admiralty and under the command of Captain John Ross explored Baffin Bay and further west in search of North west passage. In 1824 principal owners were Thomas Carlill,

Richard Waite, sailmaker, and Richard Humphreys, mariner. Captain Humphreys brought home ninety four tons of oil from five whales in 1830 and the following year under Captain McKenzie the single whale caught yielded twelve tons of oil. It was the *Isabella* under Captain Humphreys who rescued her former commander after Captain Ross and the crew of the schooner *Victory* who had set out on a voyage of exploration in 1829, was shipwrecked and lost until discovered in August 1833. *Isabella* lost in Davis Straits 1835.

James of Peterhead. 346 tons. Built at Whitby in 1811. In 1829 sold to Captain James Hogg of Peterhead, a well known whaling captain for whom Hogg's Harbour, south of Cape Searle on Baffin Island, was named. In 1830 catch of one whale yielding thirteen tons of oil. Captain Dannatt of the *Progress* of Hull lost on 2nd July first took refuge on the *James* before moving southwards from ship to ship to bring home to Hull first news of disaster in the Arctic that year. *James* lost in Melville Bay in 1831 (Captain Hogg).

John of Greenock. "Built in India of teak and doubled in London with British oak."; "a heavily built, clumsy looking craft". Captain William Scoresby senior went into partnership with Greenock merchants, when in 1811, the *John* and another large vessel were fitted out for the whaling trade, but the former soon became the sole vessel whaling out of the port. In 1816 Scoresby was succeeded as master by his son-in-law, Captain Thomas Jackson, who served until 1825. Captain Combe commanded her 1826-8, did not sail 1829 and lost in 1830.

Juno of Leith. Under command of Captain Lyall one of six ships out of Leith in 1827. In 1830 his catch was one whale yielding thirteen tons of oil; the next year four whales were caught yielding thirty tons of oil. Burnt in Lancaster Sound 1832.

Kiero of Hull. 358 tons. Built at Hull in 1811 for Egginton brothers and James Kiero Watson, banker. Under the command of Captain John Martin in 1830 her catch was three whales yielding twenty tons of oil followed by two whales yielding thirty tons of oil in 1831. Lost after 1834.

Laetitia of Aberdeen. 318 tons. Owned by Greenland Whale Fishing Company of Aberdeen in 1812. Captain Clark in command from 1819 until ship was one of four from Aberdeen lost in 1830.

Laurel of Hull. 286 tons. Built at Peterhead in 1801 and registered in Hull in 1809 to Henry Coates and Avison and John Terry, all merchants. Lost in 1830 while under the command of Captain William Manger, master from 1827.

Lee of Hull. 363 tons. Launched 1813 at Paull for William Lee and Son. In 1827 under command of Captain Lee, noted for his practice of avoiding the fleet and going his own way, usually being as well or better fished than any other in the Arctic. His was the top ship in 1830 with nine whales yielding one hundred and twenty tons of oil and again in 1831 with eleven fish making one hundred and seventy five tons of oil. Wrecked 1835 in Davis Strait.

Lord Gambier of Newcastle. Built Monkwearmouth in 1825. Registered in Hull in 1845 and Kirkcaldy in 1853. In 1831 under the command of Captain

Wareham a catch of eight whales, yielding one hundred tons of oil. Wrecked in 1863.

Madamoiselle. Captain Guedon. French whaler. A number of British seamen shipped out on French whalers in 1830. Others from wrecked ships were taken aboard. Captain North of the wrecked *William* found refuge aboard the *Madamoiselle* where he died a few days later. Many found that "French food and French discipline were not to their taste", and harsh treatment was reported.

Margaret of London. One of two ships in the London fleet in 1830 both came home clean. In 1831 Captain Fleet's catch was twenty four tons of oil from two whales – six ships in fleet. Lost in 1836 under the command of Captain Turpin ending London's whaling trade.

Middleton of Aberdeen. Two vessels of this name in Aberdeen fleet from 1813.
Middleton (I). 294 tons. In Newcastle fleet in 1801 and owned by Greenland Whale Fishing Company of Aberdeen in 1812. Lost 1830.
Middleton II. 329 tons. Built for the Union Whale Fishery Company of Aberdeen. Under the command of Captain Mills came home clean in 1830. Captain James' catch in 1831 was two whales yielding twenty four tons of oil. Lost in 1835 under Captain Kerr when forced to winter over in the Arctic.

Neptune of Aberdeen. Owned by the Union Whale Fishery Company, Aberdeen in 1804. Captain Ayrton brought home fifteen tons of oil from one whale in 1830, Captain Bruce was no more successful in 1831 with twelve tons of oil from one whale. *Neptune* left fishing for transatlantic trade in 1840.

Neptune of London. Returned home clean in 1830 and lost in 1831 under the command of Captain Wallace. Only three London ships sailed in 1832, the *Margaret* made the last voyage out of the metropolis in 1836.

North Briton of Hull. 262 tons. Built at Broad Oak, Gloucester, in 1789 for Samuel Cooper and John Marshall, major Hull whaleship owners, and Captain James Hewetson of Gainsborough on the Trent. Lost in 1830 while under the command of Captain Story. When the storm struck on 2nd July lay in the same ice dock as *Gilder*, crushed and lifted right out of the water, where they remained in plain sight for several days (see Laing's sketch).

Oxhenhope of Hull. 285 tons. Built at Selby, Yorkshire in 1803 for general trade for William Sharp, mariner and John Carlill, merchant of Hull. First whaling voyage in 1829 for owners Robert Lee and John Tall, merchants of Sculcoates, Hull. Sailed from Hull under the command of Captain McIntosh on 31st January 1830, the first whaler out of the port that ill-fated season. Lost in Melville Bay in the June.

Phoenix of Whitby. 324 tons. Captain Mills, master 1830 and 1831. Made her first voyage to the Arctic in 1816 for the owners W.T. and E. Chapman. For a number of seasons among the best fished of Davis Strait fleet. Badly stove in Melville Bay in 1830 but returned to Whitby with a catch of four whales yielding forty tons of oil. In 1831, the only whaler out of Whitby, she brought back the same tonnage from nine whales. Last voyage 1837, stranded on the outward passage.

Polar Star – Laing identifies this ship as French whaler.

Princess of Wales of Aberdeen. 308 tons. Built for the Greenland Whale Fishing Company of Aberdeen. First voyage to Arctic in 1813. Lost 1830 when Captain Gray serving first year in command. Four Aberdeen vessels lost from a fleet of ten.

Progress of Hull. In Hull fleet 1818-1830, second whaler of name. Lost 2nd July 1830 while under command of Captain Edward Dannatt her master from 1826. He made the epic journey south across the ice from ship to ship to join the *Abram* the first ship home and on 10th October brought the news to Hull of the disaster in Melville Bay.

Rambler of Kircaldy. There were five ships in Kirkcaldy fleet in 1830 and three came home clean, including the *Rambler* under the command of Captain Watson who was also the master when she was lost on 1st September 1831 during a gale.

Rattler of Leith. In Leith fleet in 1804. Her master from 1819 or earlier, Captain Stoddart, was in command in 1830 when she was one of three lost in fleet of seven ships.

Resolution of Peterhead: lost in 1830 under command of Captain Philips. The vessel had sailed in the fleet since 1813.

Resolution of Whitby. 292 tons. Built at Whitby for Captain William Scoresby (Snr.) in 1803. Sold to Captain James Hogg of Peterhead in November 1829 and sailed in 1830 under his command as one of two ships of the same name. Returned to Peterhead with ten tons of oil from a catch of one whale in 1830; in 1831 the catch was five whales producing seventy tons of oil. Fitted with a new deck and topsides in 1839. Lost in Melville Bay in 1862.

St. Andrew of Aberdeen. 313 tons. Built for the Union Whale Fishing Company of Aberdeen. First season 1813. Seriously damaged in Melville Bay in 1830. Captain Reed's catch of two whales yielded thirteen tons of oil. In 1831 he caught nine whales which yielded one hundred and ten tons of oil. Back in Aberdeen fleet in 1850; lost 1861.

Spencer of Montrose. Entered fleet in 1815. One of fleet of four when lost in 1830 while under the command of Captain Robertson who had sailed with her from 1827.

Swan of Hull. 320 tons. Built as Royal Naval vessel at Plymouth in 1767 and one of mutineer' vessels at Nore in 1797. Purchased by William Gibson, shipbuilder, Edward Gibson, merchant, and John Taylor, mariner of Hull. By 1826 in hands of Samuel and William Spyvee Cooper and Robert Draper, mariner. Captain Robert Dring, master from 1823-1840, brought her home clean in 1830, carrying aboard survivors from the *John* of Greenock. His catch in 1831 was six whales yielding ninety tons of oil. Broken up at Aberdeen in 1842.

Three Brothers of Dundee. Captain Cameron, master 1830. One of two ships lost of the Dundee fleet of nine. In the fleet since at least 1814.

Traveller of Peterhead. 401 tons. Launched in 1815 for general trade but adapted for whaling in 1821. Captain George Simpson in command from 1826 until at least 1842. Badly stove in 1830 in close proximity to the *Zephyr*, and yet brought home a catch which yielded one hundred and ten tons of oil from seven whales very close to that of the *Lee* of Hull, the best fished ship of the Arctic fleet that year. The catch included seventy butts of blubber and one and a half tons whale fins salvaged from the wreck of the *William* of Hull, the subject of an Admiralty Court enquiry in 1833. Captain Simpson brought home fifty five tons of oil from four whales in 1831 as well as bone from three fish belonging to the *James* lost that year. From the 1840s the *Traveller* always in the forefront in the taking of seals. Wrecked 1858.

Truelove of Hull. 296 tons. Built at Philadelphia in 1764 and captured during the American War of Independence. Purchased by Hull shipowners and entered the whaling trade making first voyage to the Arctic in 1784. Changes in ownership saw her employed for some years in trade. Registered to William Voase, merchant in 1810, in partnership with Thomas Hewitt, mariner, in 1825 and in the sole ownership in 1827 of Robert King. Not in the Arctic fleet in 1830 but sailed in 1831 under command of Captain William Manger, owner in partnership with Thomas and William Ward who came home with forty tons of oil from three whales. Bethel Ship until 1837 when the veteran Captain Manger ceased to be her master.
Captain John Parker took over command for the next seventeen years, many good catches and lucky escapes from destruction. A record of seventy two seasons whaling in the Arctic when in 1868 she and the *Diana* were the only two vessels in the Hull whaling trade. *Diana* lost in 1869 but the *Truelove* continued to make regular trading voyages mostly to Norway in the ice and timber trade. In 1873 to Greenland, thence to Philadelphia before sailing for Hull with a cargo of petroleum, resin and turpentine. Owned by J.S. Ward of London in 1888 and broken up sometime later.

Union of Peterhead. Her master in 1817 was Captain Mackie, who in 1830 brought home thirteen tons of oil; in 1831 his catch was four whales yielding sixty tons of oil plus six hundred seals. Lost in 1859.

Ville de Dieppe. 400 tons. Capt. Masse. Lost 1830.

William of Hull. 350 tons. Built at Sutton (Hull) in 1811. Owned from 1814 by Samuel Cooper, Tranby, and William Syvee Cooper, Sculcoates, with Thomas Hawkins, mariner and J.G. Cankrien, merchant. Captain Thomas North, master from 1828-1830. Wrecked fifty yards from the *Zephyr* in 1830; surgeon, Mr. Aitkin.

William and Ann of Whitby. In Whitby fleet 1798. One of only two ships out of Whitby in 1830 and lost under the command of Captain Terry who had taken over from Captain Smith that season.

William Lee of Hull. 376 tons. Built at Hull in 1831 for Robert Lee and John Tall, merchants. Captain Hill, master, 1831-1832, brought home forty five tons of oil from three whales in 1831 and two hundred tons of oil from twenty seven whales the following year. She served in the whaling fleet until 1836 and restored direct trade from Hull to India in 1838. Lost in 1847.

William Torr of Hull. 281 tons. Built at Hull in 1821 for Thomas Torr, George Rudston, linen draper, and Phillip Dannatt, mariner. William Torr of Riby Grove, Lincolnshire also a shareholder in 1825. Captain Dannatt was her master from 1821 to 1834 and brought home eighty tons of oil from five whales in 1830 and one hundred and thirty tons of oil from thirteen whales the following year. Lost under the command of Captain Snaith in 1835.

13. NOTES

1. Cited in Sanderson, John. *A voyage from Hull to Greenland in the ship SAMUEL in the year 1789 ...* Kingston Upon Hull, p. 18-19.
2. Laing John. *An account of a voyage to Spitzbergen; containing A Full Description of that Country, of The Zoology of the North, and of the Shetland Isles; with an Account of the Whale Fishery.* London, printed for J. Mawman, London; and David Brown, Edinburgh, 1815 p. 138.
3. There was apparently another surgeon Dr. John Laing with Newburgh associations. The only information uncovered to date with regard to this contemporary of the son of Peter Laing relates to property in Newburgh transferred in 1833 and 1834 to the former's children then living in Surrey, England. Ref: *Newburgh Minute Book of Sassines,* 1822.
4. Information on life in the town and its surroundings is based on several sources, primarily *Lindores Abbey and its Burgh of Newburgh Their History and Annals* by Alexander Laing, published in Edinburgh in 1876. A cousin of George and probably nephew of John. Alexander Laing (1808-1892), a banker by profession but historian and antiquarian by inclination, made this detailed study of the district which earned him an honorary doctorate from St. Andrews University. A bachelor, his legacy of a building now known as the Laing Museum, houses the bequest of his library and antiquarian collection of the fellow townsmen whose welfare was his lifelong concern.

    Captain John Wilson, descendant of John Wilson, schoolmaster of the Parish School at Newburgh from about 1776 whose post was taken over by his son James until the latter's death in 1859, has generously shared his great knowledge of Newburgh and its people, as well as enabling me to visualise the nature of early land division in the burgh by taking me down a passage between two houses in Main Street into a long, narrow, terraced rear garden stretching to the burgh boundary. The orchard was kept in the tradition of fruit growing begun by the monks of Lindores Abbey.
5. Rev. Thomas Stuart in *The Statistical Account of Scotland Drawn up from the Communications of the ministers of the Parishes.* Edinburgh. 1793, p. 180.
6. On the Mugdrum Estate. Ref: G. Wilson, Curator, Laing Museum, Newburgh, Fife, personal communication 18th August 1988.

    Fishing stations were let each year by public auction held at the West Port at Newburgh. The tacksmen who rented the fishing owned their own nets and boats, and by 1790 a big trade had developed as four sailing cutters crewed by Newburgh men transported the salmon, either packed in ice or salted, to London. Information provided by Captain John Wilson, Newburgh. Stuart, op.cit has comment on the nature and importance of the trade, p. 172.

7.   Martin P. *Newburgh. A short history and Guided walk,* p. 9. She quotes the Minister of Abdie, 1791.
8.   See Forster, H. *The Mariana Islands, 1830-1831. From the Journal of John Lyell on the Whaleship "Ranger"* in *ISLA: A Journal of Micronesian Studies,* Dry Season, 1992, p. 355-387.
9.   Information supplied by the Royal College of Surgeons of England, 21st July 1993.
10.   He again matriculated in medicine in the sessions 1814-15, 1816-17 during which time ... *Voyage to Spitzbergen* was published. Ref: Information provided by Miss J. Currie, Edinburgh University Library, 20th July 1993.
In his letter to William Scoresby Jnr. date 12th February 1807 John Laing wrote ... "I have a great many patients who are not perfectly recovered and consequently I have not rec'd my charges and should I go away, I would in a great measure lose my money ...my wife is very importunate with regard to my staying at home, lest we should fall in with some of Bonaparte's pirates". Ref: Scoresby Archives, Whitby Literary and Philosophical Society, Yorkshire.
11.   There is no record of his having graduated from Edinburgh University. In his application to St. Andrews University for a M.D., John Laing identifies himself as the son of Peter Laing, merchant, of Newburgh, which establishes his relationship to George Laing. His referees were John Barclay and Alexander Logie. Ref: B. Smart, keeper of MSS and Muniments at St. Andrews University via J. Poole, 2nd Feb. 1995.
12.   Morrell, J.B. *Medicine and science in the Eighteenth century* in *Four centuries* ... edited by G. Donaldson, p. 51.
13.   Laing, J. op cit, p. 149-152.
14.   Ibid., p. 152
15.   The experience of Dr. John Wilson expressed in a journal kept while serving as surgeon aboard the London whaleship *Gipsy* on a voyage to the Pacific, 1839-1843. Ref: *The cruise of the GIPSY – The Journal of John Wilson, Surgeon of a whaling voyage to the Pacific Ocean* 1839-43 edited by H. Forster, 1991.
16.   Laing, J. *op.cit,* p.1.
17.   Miss A.M. Stevenson, Royal College of Surgeons of Edinburgh to J.S., 22nd September 1993.
18.   He died on 23rd September 1832, aged 59. On the gravestone are 'the names of his wife, Elizabeth Davidson; their children, Elizabeth who died at 10, and William at 3; of his second wife, Christina Elizabeth Gib; and of John, his only son by the latter, who died at 22.' There was a daughter Margaret. Ref: *Memorials of St. Michaels. The Old Parish Churchyard of Dumfries* by W. McDowell. Edinburgh, Adam & Charles Black, 1876.
19.   Forster, H. *The Mariana Isles ... op.cit,* p.382. Lyell married Ann Williamson of Cluniefield in 1835. George Laing's Mother was also Ann Williamson, born a generation earlier at Adbie which suggests a relationship.
20.   Biddle, G. and O.S. Nock. *The railway heritage of Britain,* p. 15; Ellis, C. H. *The North British Railway,* p. 31.
21.   General Census 1851.

22. *The Medical Register*, 1876.

23. Reported in *Fifeshire Journal, 29th January 1863*, p.6.

24. The entry for 13th May 1809 in the journal of William Scoresby Junior records this description of "what is called "whale bone" consisting of thin parallel lamina, ... of a fibrous texture. It is composed of hair of which the inside of the bone is covered ...In some fish the whalebone is straight, in others considerably curved. The largest blades are not exactly in the middle and in a full grown fish would be from ten to thirteen feet in length. Towards each end they decrease in length. In each side there are about three hundred blades of bone". Ref: Stamp, T. and C. *Greenland Voyager*. Whitby, 1983, p. 123.

In John Laing's time a whale was called a "payable or sizeable fish" when the longest of the laminae was found to be at least six feet in length when, "for every one of which that is caught, the captain generally get three guineas, the surgeon one, the carpenter one, etc." Ref: *An account of a voyage to Spitzbergen,* 1815, p. 125.

25. The enterprising advertisers took the opportunity of promoting their wares by printing an "Extract from the last address of the Board of Agriculture", by Sir John Sinclair, Bart, on the 7th June 1808. "The Whalebone sieves & nets for confining sheep, Invented by Mr Bowman, are evidently much more durable, & in other respects greatly to be preferred, desirable also, by increasing the consumption of Whalebone, to promote our fisheries, which, like other branches of domestic industry, cannot be too much encouraged." Handbill held at Hull Maritime Museum and reproduced in an article by T. Sheppard in *The Mariners Mirror*, vol. VI, no. 5, p. 186.

26. Quoted from *An account of the Arctic regions* by William Scoresby Jnr. published in 1820 in *William Scoresby Arctic Scientist* (1976) by Tom and Cordelia Stamp. p. 12.

27. Sheppard and Suddaby, op. cit., p. 11.

28. A.G. Credland, personal communication.

29. *Gentleman's Magazine*, 1830, pt.2, p. 392.

30. Sheppard and Suddaby, *Hull whaling relics* etc., 1906, p. 15.

31. A.G. Credland, personal communication, 13th April 1992.

32. Captain McIntosh of the *Oxenhope* stole a march on Captain Lee of the *Lee,* who for a number of years had been the first whaleman to head out from Hull for the season. In 1830 he sailed on 1st February. Lubbock, B. *The Arctic whalers,* p. 278.

33. Laing, J. op. cit., p. 7.

34. Bourmaster appears to be an unusual forename as there is no such term in the whaleman's vocabulary.

35. "The work of the best medical men in Edinburgh". C Cowen, D.L. *The early years of the Edinburgh Medical School.*

36. Lubbock, B. op. cit. p. 12.

37. Sheppard and Suddaby. op. cit. p. 11-12.

38. An unnamed surgeon who served on the *Hercules* of Aberdeen in 1831 writes that during a few days of "beautifully serene weather" with about thirty sail in company, he enjoyed the experience of ships towing in competition – of

hearing the sounds of the men roaring out their shanties, of tracking pipes playing and skippers "howling" orders from the masthead as they urged their toiling crewmen to greater effort. Ref: Journal held at King's College, Aberdeen. Lubbock (op. cit., p. 56) also records such occasions.

39, 40. These experiences are extracted from letters incorporated in a contemporary report of the disaster published in the *Chronicle for 1830* under the heading *Davis Straits Fishing* in *The Annual Register,* vol LXXII, p. 153.

41.   Lubbock, B. *op. cit.*, p. 279-80.

42.   Same source as notes 39 and 40.

43.   *Ibid.*

44.   *Ibid.*, p. 294.

45.   Lubbock, p. 284. Sheppard and Suddaby, p. 15;

46.   Information supplied by A. G. Credland.

47.   Norwegian Danish colonization of Greenland began in 1721. The settlement at Upernavik was established in 1771, and by 1800 all of West Greenland had been "included under permanent rule." Ref: *Greenland seen through fifty years of stamps 1938-1988.* Copenhagen, 1989, p. 56-7.

48.   Ref: Lubbock, B. op. cit., p. 283 and Chatterton, E.K. *Whales and whaling*, p. 58-9. The surgeon of the *Hercules* in 1834 writes of coming across her scattered wreck. There appears to be very little known of the whole sorry episode.

49.   Illustrated with pen and ink sketches the original journal is held at King's College, Aberdeen.

50.   Shipping and trade in and out of Greenland became a Danish government monopoly from 1774 with skins and blubber the main commodities traded for European articles "like firearms, iron, coffee, tobacco and clothes." Ref: *Greenland* ...

The Inuit were shrewd traders and recognised that the whalers "eagerly sought after" what they had to offer – skins, blubber, tusks etc. which they exchanged for iron, tools, needles, and porcelain. Clothing was often exchanged. Those moving amongst the whaling ships had enough English to make themselves understood.

51.   The surgeon sketches these buttons and other artefacts. *Inuit* is the plural of *Inuk* the word for person or human being in the language of Eskimo.

52.   Constant struggle for survival on a minimum level is a commonly held view of the nature of Inuit society, but in the opinion of a group of Danish physical anthropologists "Inuit society has survived by being able to live in and with the cold and not by struggling against it". Ref: A chapter headed *The people* in *The Greenland Mummies*, published in English in 1991, published in English in 1991, p. 66.

53.   The medical men consulted offered diagnoses similar to that of George Laing's great grandson, Dr. David Laing, who suggests "a traumatic haemarthrosis of the right shoulder with ... fractured ribs displaced through intense physical activity irritating the pleura with the possibility of a minor rupture of the lung giving the patient very painful respiratory excursions". He found the most interesting aspect of "this fortunate fellow's injuries" to be "the quaint treatments embarked upon". A second opinion offered the possibility of mercury poisoning from an overuse of calomel, while a third suggested "gross over medication".

14. BIBLIOGRAPHY

M. Adlard, *The Greenlander*, London, Penguin Books, 1978.

G. Biddle and O.S. Nock, *The railway heritage of Britain*, London, Michael Joseph, 1983.

A. R. Buchan, *The Peterhead whaling trade*, Peterhead, The Buchan Field Club. Occasional paper No. 1, 1993.

W. E. Cass. The Journal of Surgeon Cass aboard the whaler BRUNSWICK of Hull, 1824, Hull 1988. Edited A.G. Credland *Humberside Heritage Publication, No. 18.*

E. K. Chatterton, *Whales and whaling*, London, Philip Allan and Co. 1930.

D. L. Cowen *The Edinburgh Pharmacopoeia* in *The early years of the Edinburgh Medical School*, Edinburgh, the Royal Scottish Museum, 1976.

Arthur G. Credland 'The Hull Whaling Trade – an Arctic Enterprise'. Hutton Press, Cherry Burton 1995.

C. H. Ellis, *The North British Railway*, London, Ian Allan, 1995.

H. Forster, ed., *The cruise of the Gipsy – The Journal of John Wilson, Surgeon on a whaling voyage to the Pacific Ocean, 1839-43*, Ye Galleon Press, Washington 1991.

Greenland seen through fifty years of Stamps 1938-1988, Copenhagen, the Greenland Post office 1989.

C. B. Gunn, *Leaves from the life of a country doctor* (edited by R. Crockett) Edinburgh, The Ettrick Press, 1947.

D. Guthrie, *The medical school of Edinburgh*, Edinburgh 1959.

J. P. Hart Hansen, J. Meldgaard, J. and J. Nordquist., eds. *The Greenland Mummies.* London, British Museum Press, 1991. First published in Danish by The Greenland Museum, Nuuk and Christian Elgars Forlag, Copenhagen, 1985.

D. B. Horn, *A short history of the University of Edinburgh*, Edinburgh, The University Press, 1967.

G. Jackson, *The British whaling trade,* London, Adam and Charles Black, 1978.

A. Laing, *Lindores Abbey and its Burgh of Newburgh. Their History and Annals,* Edinburgh Edmonston and Douglas, 1876.

J. Laing, *An account of a voyage to Spitzbergen: containing a Full Description of that Country, of the Zoology of the North, and of the Shetland Isles; with an Account of the Whale Fishery.* London, printed for J. Mawman, London; and David Brown, Edinburgh, 1815.

B. Lubbock, *The Arctic whalers*, Glasgow, Brown, Son & Ferguson, 1978.

P. Martin, Newburgh. *A short history and guided walk.* Peat Inn, Fife, The Author, 1992.

J. B. Morrell, *Medicine and science in the Eighteenth century in Four centuries* ... (edited by G. Donaldson), Edinburgh, University of Edinburgh, 1983.

J. Sanderson, *A voyage from Hull to Greenland in the ship SAMUEL in the year 1789* ... Kingston Upon Hull: printed for the Author by T. Briggs, and sold by W. Bell, E. Foster, and W. Mowatt, Booksellers, [n.d.]

T. Sheppard, and J. Suddaby. *Hull whaling relics and Arctic or historical records of 250 years*, published as Hull Museum Publication, No 31, Hull, 1906.

Robert Smith, *The whale hunters*, Edinburgh, John Donald Publishers, 1993.

T. C. Smout and Sydney Wood. *Scottish voices 1745-1960.* Collins, London, 1990.

T. and C. Stamp, *Greenland Voyager*, Whitby, Caedmon of Whitby Press, 1983

T. and C. Stamp, *William Scoresby. Arctic scientist*, Whitby, Caedmon of Whitby Press, 1993.

T. Stuart, *Parish of Newburgh in The Statistical Account of Scotland drawn from the communications of the Ministers of the Different Parishes, Edinburgh, 1793.*

P. J. Wallis, and R. V. Wallis. *Eighteenth century medics,* Newcastle upon Tyne Project for Historical Bibliography, 1988.

R. C. Wright-St. Clair, *Thoroughly a man of the world.* A biography of Sir David Monro. Christchurch, Whitcombe and Tombs, 1971.

Periodicals

The Annual Register or a view of the History, Politics and Literature of the year 1830, vol. LXXII. London, 1830.

Fifeshire Journal.

Gentleman's Magazine, 1830.

The Mariners Mirror, vol. 6, no. 5, p. 186.

The Medical Register 1876.